Reading Comprehension Workbook

Level 9

Series Designer

Philip J. Solimene

Editor

Sharon Diane Orlan

Reading Consultant

Sidney J. Rauch, Ed.D.

Professor of Reading and Education
Hofstra University, New York

EDCON

Long Island, N.Y.

Story Authors
Ruth W. Barrett
Jackson Daviss
William W. Hull
Hazel Krantz
Barbara LaMonica
Naila Miniai
Margaret Opsata
Deborah Tiersch-Allen

Printed in U.S.A.
ISBN# 0-931334-38-1

CONTENTS

CONTENTS

Full Steam Ahead!

Learn the Key Words

amputate (am′ pyə tāt) to cut off from the body
The doctor was about to amputate the sailor's leg.

belligerent (bə lij′ ər ənt) warlike or hostile
The belligerent vessel was flying a Confederate flag.

concede (kən sēd′) to surrender; yield
The enemy commander had to concede to superior forces.

converge (kən vėrj′) to come together; to move toward the same place
The ships were about to converge on the enemy.

decisive (di sī′ siv) referring to a clear decision; beyond doubt
Washington's army achieved a decisive victory over the British troops.

ravage (rav′ ij) to damage violently or destroy
The soldiers in the fort knew the ships' big guns would ravage the walls.

Preview:
1. Read the title.
2. Look at the picture.
3. Read the first six paragraphs of the selection.
4. Then answer the following question.

You learned from your preview that
_____a. Billy Watson was in command of the Hartford.
_____b. there was a total of seventeen ships in the squadron.
_____c. the incident took place in the nineteenth century.
_____d. the Tennessee was preparing to converge on the Hartford and two other ships.

Turn to the Comprehension Check on page 4 for the right answer.

Now read the selection.

Read to find out about an important event in our history.

1

Full Steam Ahead!

On the morning of August 5, 1864, Union and Confederate warships were preparing to engage in one of the most dramatic sea battles in history.

"Put her hard over, Mr. Thompson," said the commanding officer of U.S.S. Hartford to his second in command," we're going in close to starboard, if you please."

"Aye, sir!" answered Lieutenant Thompson, raising a metal speaking tube to his lips and relaying the command to the two sailors steering two of her sister ships that were about to converge on the Confederate ironclad, Tennessee. The Lieutenant had to use the metal megaphone so he could be heard over the sounds of battle raging around them.

A young sailor, Billy Watson, heard the command and looked across the water toward the threatening ironclad and then back at Rear Admiral Farragut standing near the Captain. As he stared, he fingered the lucky five dollar gold piece his brother had given him when he enlisted.

He heard the Captain speak again. "Let her fall off just a bit, Mr. Thompson, and ready the port guns."

"Aye, sir!" said the Lieutenant. "Three points to starboard!" he ordered the men at the helm,

then turned his horn toward the gun deck and shouted, "Attention on deck! Bring your guns to bear and fire on command!"

It was nine o'clock on the bright, sunny morning of August 5, 1864. The Hartford and seventeen other ships in the squadron had been fighting the Confederate navy and firing on their forts for more than three hours, and neither side was willing to concede.

At five-thirty that morning they had moved in from the Gulf of Mexico and made a sweep from the west of the narrow peninsula, across the mouth of Mobile Bay and the eastern end of the closest island. The Southerners had built forts on the tips of the peninsula and island near the bay entrance. Some of the ships were able to move in near the forts on the Gulf side and their guns had been enough to ravage the fort walls. They had raked them with murderous fire, silencing them quickly. Then the Hartford, flagship of the flotilla, took the lead, moving into the bay. Rear Admiral David Farragut led his ships between the ravaged forts

and the battle began in earnest.

The Union sailors were all aware of the terrible chance they were taking as they sailed into the mouth of the bay. The word-of-mouth telegraph among the sailors reported that the Confederates had placed explosives in the water near the entrance of the bay. They were called torpedoes and were used like mines. Consisting of cylinders of boiler iron filled with gun powder, they were suspended under sealed casks and barrels which floated on top of the water. The larger ones weighed as much as 2,000 pounds, but were difficult to spot because they floated so low. They would explode on contact with ships that ran into them. Because their ports were being blockaded, the Confederates used more torpedoes than the Union navy. Billy remembered hearing that only three months before, a torpedo had sunk a 542 ton gunboat on the James River in Virginia.

After entering the bay, and even before they had a chance to exchange shots with the Confederate ships, Billy and his shipmates had watched helplessly as the U.S.S. Tecumseh hit a torpedo and sank, drowning 93 of her crew. Farragut seemed unafraid of the danger, and he gave an order to steam full speed ahead. Hearing this fearless command had given the men and officers a feeling of pride, and in spite of concern about the torpedoes, they continued to steam toward the Confederate ships and into the battle. Until now, neither side had any decisive victories; they merely had reduced the number of vessels involved.

Several ships had gotten successfully by the torpedoes and had engaged the enemy. There hadn't been a single man hurt on the flagship, but the other Union ships had lost 145 men and there were 170 wounded on their decks. And now, the flagship was bearing down on the most dangerous vessel in the Confederate navy.

Billy was a "powder monkey," a name given to the sailors who ran buckets of powder between the deck guns and the powder storage bins. It was an exhausting and dangerous job during a battle, but Billy didn't mind. He had been under fire before and was proud to be serving on the same ship with Admiral Farragut who would never concede defeat. He felt that as long as he was so near the Admiral and had his lucky coin, even the belligerent and much feared ironclad Tennessee couldn't hurt him.

Three Union ships had already rammed the giant ironclad and now Billy's ship was moving in to finish it off.

A shout from an officer sent Billy hurrying below deck for more powder as his ship pulled ahead of the others and engaged the pride of the enemy's navy in close combat with its big guns.

When Billy got back on deck, the Tennessee was out of control because it had lost its rudder. It was a dangerous situation because of the number of ships close by and the debris floating around them. At that very moment, the Confederate Admiral was lying below deck with a badly mangled leg caused by a shell propelled by Billy's last bucket of powder. A ship's doctor was trying to decide if he would have to amputate it.

The Captain of the Tennessee was vainly trying to get his engines reversed so he could move away from the battle and repair his rudder, but all he managed to do was turn broadside to the swiftly converging Hartford. His port guns had been damaged and they now lay quietly, out of action.

Mobile Bay was shaped like a giant triangle about thirty miles long and reached all the way up to the major city of Mobile, Alabama, at its northern point. Billy knew that if they won the battle today, the Federal troops already outside of Mobile could move in and another Confederate city would be in Northern hands.

Billy gave his lucky coin another rub as he scrambled down the companionway toward the storage bin for more powder. Just then the Tennessee smashed into the Hartford, throwing him to the deck. At almost the same moment, the gunnery officer gave the order to fire. The Hartford's shots ripped through the armor plates of the Tennessee and before Billy emerged on deck again, the ironclad was signaling its surrender.

A shout went up from the crew as the belligerent metal ship, said to be the most powerful ironclad afloat, conceded defeat and lowered its colors. It was only ten o'clock in the morning and the Union had won the day. Even though they had more deaths than the Confederates, they had captured 270 of the enemy and the Confederate Admiral was out of action, facing the possible amputation of his leg.

The previous night the flotilla had waited out in the Gulf. Billy had taken this opportunity to write a letter to his brother. A piece of planking he had borrowed from a ship's carpenter served as a lap desk upon which to write by candlelight in the crew's quarters. Scribbling with the broken stub of a pencil, he had written his brother all about his serving on the flagship of the popular Farragut and the possibility of a sea battle the next day. Billy reminded his brother that he still had the gold piece and that he hoped to carry it into Mobile Bay the next morning.

At the same time, occupying more spacious quarters far above Billy's head, the Admiral himself was also writing a letter. He wrote to his wife: "In the morning, if 'God is my leader' as I hope He is, I'm going into Mobile Bay."

When Admiral Farragut entered Mobile Bay the following day, he scored a decisive victory for the Union forces.

Full Steam Ahead!

COMPREHENSION CHECK

Preview Answer:

c. the incident took place in the nineteenth century.

Choose the best answer.

1. The Union sailors were taking a risk by sailing into the mouth of the bay because the
   ____a. Confederates had submarines hidden under the deep water.
   ____b. bay was shallow and they might run aground there.
   ____c. Confederates had planted torpedoes under the water.
   ____d. U.S.S. Hartford was damaged and sinking fast.

2. A "powder monkey"
   ____a. climbed through the corridors of the engine room making repairs.
   ____b. supplied buckets of gun powder to various decks on the ship.
   ____c. was a kind of mascot aboard the U.S.S. Hartford.
   ____d. was the lowest-ranking sailor aboard a Confederate ship.

3. First, the Tennessee lost its rudder. Then, in an effort to steer it away from the Hartford, the Captain turned the Tennessee broadside to the approaching ship. Next,
   ____a. the Captain of the Tennessee surrendered.
   ____b. the Hartford fired on the Tennessee.
   ____c. the Tennessee smashed into the Hartford.
   ____d. the Tennessee sunk instantly.

4. The Hartford's battle with the Tennessee in Mobile Bay would
   ____a. have no effect on the land war at all.
   ____b. be more of a risk than it was worth.
   ____c. have an important effect on the war effort.
   ____d. have made the Captain very famous.

5. The U.S.S. Hartford was
   ____a. an honored ship because Admiral Farragut was on board.
   ____b. just another member of the Union fleet.
   ____c. in poor condition to enter a battle.
   ____d. not staffed to its fullest capacity.

6. Billy believed in the admiral because he
   ____a. was like the father that Billy had back home.
   ____b. was a treasured friend of his brother's.
   ____c. had proven himself trustworthy and courageous.
   ____d. was a great politician and statesman.

7. The atmosphere on the Hartford as it entered into battle was
   ____a. confident but thoughtful.
   ____b. energetic, but sad.
   ____c. tranquil and serene.
   ____d. violent and charged.

8. The admiral was
   ____a. always absolutely sure that he would win.
   ____b. not really as sure as he led his men to believe.
   ____c. never able to command respect from the men.
   ____d. a quiet man who made few important decisions.

9. Another name for this selection could be
   ____a. "Victory in Mobile Bay."
   ____b. "The Confederacy Moves In."
   ____c. "Homeward Bound."
   ____d. "A Sailor's Dream."

10. This selection is mainly about
    ____a. a young man in battle aboard a flagship of the Union fleet.
    ____b. an admiral who did not know when to stop fighting and retreat.
    ____c. a bay that is in the shape of a giant triangle with the most treacherous conditions.
    ____d. a young man who relies on his brother to give him confidence in difficult situations.

11. *Develop your own sentences using any four key words found in the box on the following page.*

1. _____

2. _____

3. _____

4. _____

Check your answers with the key on page 53.

Full Steam Ahead!

VOCABULARY CHECK

amputate	belligerent	concede	converge	decisive	ravage

I. Fill in the blank in each sentence with the correct key word from the box above.

1. The doctor was forced to _____ the carpenter's finger after it had been crushed beyond repair.

2. The troops had been given orders to _____ the enemy stations.

3. The salesman's _____ attitude angered the shoppers so much that they left the store without buying anything.

4. The boxer will _____ his title if he loses the match.

5. The locusts will _____ on farmers' crops and devour them.

6. Winning at Mobile Bay was a _____ victory for the Union fleet.

II. Are the following key words used correctly in each sentence? Check yes or no.

1. The belligerent athlete provoked shouts of hostility from the spectators.
   _____Yes   _____No
2. The police planned to converge on the hideout from all possible directions.
   _____Yes   _____No
3. The surgeon was going to amputate the infected leg by repairing it.
   _____Yes   _____No
4. The commander told the forces to concede and continue to fight.
   _____Yes   _____No
5. The starving hunters had to ravage a nearby food hut.
   _____Yes   _____No
6. Anesthesia was a decisive gain in the field of medicine.
   _____Yes   _____No

Check your answers with the key on page 55.

The Market Street Massacre

Learn the Key Words

antagonize   (an tag′ ə nīz)   to arouse dislike; make an enemy of
The saleslady's persistence only served to <u>antagonize</u> Anne.

arrogant   (ar′ ə gent)   excessively proud and contemptuous of others
Even though Jack received a promotion, he did not become <u>arrogant</u>.

comply   (kəm plī)   act in agreement with a request or command
When you sign a contract, you must <u>comply</u> with the requirements.

deliberate   (di lib′ ər it)   intended; purposely done or said
Mark made a <u>deliberate</u> attempt to avoid telling Frank the truth.

fatality   (fā tal′ ə tē)   a death resulting from an accident or disaster
There was only one <u>fatality</u> as a result of the heavy snowfall.

suppress   (sə pres′)   to subdue; to hold back
The soldiers were on guard to <u>suppress</u> a rebellion.

Preview:
1. Read the title.
2. Look at the picture.
3. Read the first five paragraphs of the selection.
4. Then answer the following question.

You learned from your preview that
_____a. there is a hurricane coming.
_____b. Carlos is an aggressive shopkeeper.
_____c. the shopkeepers were used to this kind of action.
_____d. Prohibition was illegal.

Turn to the Comprehension Check on page 9 for the right answer.

Now read the selection.
Read to find out about a fictional event that really could have happened.

The Market Street Massacre

Something you will read about:

Prohibition (prō ə bish′ ən) a period between 1920 and 1933 when the sale of liquor was forbidden

Violence and fear had become a part of everyday life—When would it end?

With the force of a small hurricane, the gorilla-like man shoved Carlos into a display of canned goods, and the grocer as well as the groceries tumbled to the floor.

"My boss wants his money tomorrow and unless he gets it, your shelves will look like firewood," proclaimed the bulky, arrogant man.

Then he turned and shuffled out of the store in a manner that suggested business as usual. Carlos's expression was one of silent indignation as he added this threat to the many on his ever-growing list.

There was no definite way to conquer the evils that Prohibition had created. It seemed that as soon as something became illegal and difficult to obtain, there arose an extraordinary number of ways to smuggle, steal or make it because the challenge was rewarded by an enormous profit.

Now Carlos and the merchants of Market Street were caught in a power struggle between two of the most influential east side bosses, and paying "protection" had become a natural part of the shopkeepers' lives. Carlos paid Fat Sam and his boys to insure against the possibility that any harm might come to his meager establishment. But in reality, Carlos was paying Fat Sam not to inflict the harm that the grocer feared so intensely.

Carlos rose to his feet and began to tuck in his shirt and straighten his apron. As he brushed the dust marks off his apron he was confronted by another hulk of a man. The face was a familiar but troublesome one.

"Mr. Mancini?" There was an air of concern in the visitor's voice. "What is going on here?" questioned Joey, even though he knew all too well.

Carlos stared into Joey's eyes with disgust and humiliation.

"What do you want from me, Joey? How much does your Mr. Jim want this time?"

Joey was not surprised by the grocer's arrogant reaction, as he stood quietly before the elderly man. Joey's father had owned a store on Market Street until his death five years ago. The old man had offered his son the store and all that went with it, but the young man had plans of his own. Joey had a soft heart to match his soft head and was easily directed into the less than honest operations of Big Jim. With lots of concentrated effort, Joey worked himself up to a "respectable" position in Jim's organization, but now his uglier responsibilities were taking him directly to his father's old friends on Market Street.

"Jim wants fifty for starters, Mr. Mancini," said Joey. "I kept him down to only fifty," he repeated as if it was some kind of favor for which the grocer should thank him.

Carlos could not suppress his hostility. "Tell your Mr. Jim that I will not pay!"

Joey shook his head back and forth slowly in a way that told Carlos without words that his reply was neither a healthy nor a wise one.

That night the shopkeeper received phone calls from two of his friends on Market Street. Frank, the cafe owner, reported that he had two visitors whose sole purpose was to antagonize him, so he paid them both for the sake of his family. Tony, the barber, went to the other extreme and refused to comply with the demands of either of his un-welcomed guests.

The next morning when Carlos arrived at his grocery store, he found that every pane of glass had been knocked out and crushed into the tiniest pieces so that not even the smallest section was able to be repaired.

Tears of frustration veiled his eyes and Carlos was filled with an anger that swelled within him more each minute as he gazed upon the senseless and deliberate destruction. All he could think about was how hard he had worked to have something of his own, and now it was no longer his. As Carlos began to sweep the bits of broken glass into a box, he had no way of knowing that the worst was yet to be discovered.

Screams rang out from down the block and the police sirens began to sound. Carlos dashed from behind the counter out into the street to find the wife of Tony, the barber, in an uncontrollable condition. Tony had left his house last night to do some walking and some thinking. The barber had taken refuge in his small shop where he could sit alone surrounded by all of the things that had become so much a part of himself for so many years. Tony's peaceful moments were destroyed by the terrorist activities of the gangsters, and the barber became just another fatality in just another violent episode.

When Joey arrived at the grocery store that day, Carlos spit at him.

"That is for the disgusting, deplorable animals with whom you join forces. That is for the poor excuse of a man you have become!" shouted the grocer, his face twisted with anger.

Joey kept his eyes on the floor.

Overcome with embarrassment and a clear sense of failure, Joey meant to clear his guilt-ridden conscience by offering the shopkeepers of Market Street an alternative.

"Mr. Mancini," began the young man, his head still bowed, "Fat Sam and Big Jim will be meeting you at Frank's cafe tomorrow at one o'clock to talk 'peace.' I propose that you and your friends give them a taste of

their own medicine. Keep the secret among yourselves, but organize your forces and I will supply the weapons."

The grocer's eyes widened and a peculiar smile came across his face. He knew that his comrades would be happy to comply with the young man's offer. The two big bosses would not be able to antagonize the men of Market Street any more. Even though Carlos believed that he had to protect himself, deep down inside he felt that violence was not right. He also believed that he had no choice but to fight back.

It was a bitter cold afternoon, and the dreary winter sky hinted that snow would soon begin to fall. At precisely one o'clock, one black limousine pulled up to the curb in front of Frank's cafe, and moments later, a second limousine appeared on the other-wise deserted street. The bodyguards opened the doors and the occupants got out. When the men were finally seated at a specially chosen table, the guards took their proper places. Then, from the back, emerged Carlos and the other merchants. Joey appeared from a poorly lit side doorway.

"Since this is a peace talk," he addressed the group, "and since you are all gentlemen, I must ask you to surrender your weapons to me."

Fat Sam and Big Jim looked at each other and nodded in agreement. They laid their weapons on the table and instructed their bodyguards to do the same.

"Thank you gentlemen," said Joey, very sincerely.

Carlos and his friends cast glances among themselves and smiled, happily anticipating the surprise attack. Joey was truly on their side.

Joey asked Carlos and the other merchants to be seated and then he began the conference.

"Gentlemen, the time has come for the hatred and the violence to stop. We can gain nothing from the killings and, quite frankly, we can all benefit by joining our forces."

Carlos and the merchants looked at each other, confused and angry.

"But what about . . ." Carlos

started to rise from his seat as he addressed Joey.

"Mr. Mancini," Joey said quietly, "I only *told* you that I would provide you with weapons so that you would come to this meeting. You would never have come otherwise."

"But they *deserve* to die!" Carlos could not suppress his anger and the other merchants agreed loudly.

"No one *deserves* to die, Mr. Mancini," Joey jumped up from his chair and shouted back. "Besides, since when do two wrongs make a right? The killings and fatalities would only continue. You deliberately kill their men, they kill yours...Is this what you want? Someone has to stop it!"

Carlos sat down and the men at the table grew silent. They all turned towards Joey.

"All right," he said calmly, "now let's get started."

He was comforted in knowing that, at the very least, he had managed to get these men together. It was a start.

After hours of heated discussion, they finally arrived at an agreement, which Joey put in written form. Fat Sam and Big Jim would help the merchants repair their establishments and would protect them from outside forces. In return, the merchants would take a portion of their profits every week, and, together with the bosses' finances, would put all of the money toward a community project.

Joey presented the agreement to the gathering for all to read. Fat Sam picked up a pen, signed his name and handed the pen to Big Jim, who did the same. Then Carlos silently asked the other merchants for their opinions. Nodding affirmatively, Carlos accepted the pen from Big Jim and signed his name. The other men signed also.

Things were not going to be easy, and the project would take a long time, but it was worth it.

The Market Street Massacre

COMPREHENSION CHECK

Choose the best answer.

1. Prohibition made
____a. liquor sales illegal.
____b. voting illegal.
____c. cafes illegal.
____d. gambling illegal.

2. Joey was
____a. basically a good man.
____b. a man with no conscience.
____c. a very intelligent businessman.
____d. the son of Tony the barber.

3. The organization tried to force Carlos to pay by
____a. kidnapping his children and wife.
____b. beating him and damaging his store.
____c. stealing his merchandise and money.
____d. taking over his small grocery store.

4. The author's purpose for writing this selection was to show that
____a. killers are really nice people at heart.
____b. liquor sales are important to society.
____c. too much power in the wrong hands is a deadly thing.
____d. small businesses do not last long.

5. First, the gangsters threatened each of the merchants. Then, the shopkeepers discussed their terrible plight. Next,
____a. Carlos found his windows destroyed.
____b. Fat Sam's boy roughed up the shopkeeper.
____c. Joey was found dead.
____d. the limousines arrived at the cafe.

6. Carlos was a
____a. cowardly grocery store owner.
____b. fearless, nasty man.
____c. conceited and prosperous store owner.
____d. a man of principles and reality.

7. According to the selection, which of the following was *not* a result of Fat Sam's and Big Jim's influence?
____a. Tony the barber's death
____b. A rise in taxes
____c. Peace negotiations
____d. A ruined grocery store

8. The shopkeepers
____a. were torn between two bosses.
____b. made trouble for themselves.
____c. were in a very beneficial situation.
____d. should have ignored the gangsters.

9. Another name for this selection could be
____a. "Mobsters and Men."
____b. "A Charming Cafe."
____c. "Hope for the Future."
____d. "Joey Loses His Fight."

10. This selection is mainly about
____a. shopkeepers and their fight against crime.
____b. illegal liquor sales in a small cafe on Market Street.
____c. Joey's effort to atone for his poor manners.
____d. a man who killed others for the pure pleasure of it.

11.   *Develop your own sentences using any four key words found in the box on the following page.*
1. _____
2. _____
3. _____
4. _____

Check your answers with the key on page 53.

The Market Street Massacre

VOCABULARY CHECK

| antagonize | arrogant | comply | deliberate | fatality | suppress |

I. *Fill in the blank in each sentence with the correct key word from the box above.*

1. A bull fighter attempts to _____ the bull with his red cape.

2. The _____ man degraded his opponent in a cruel manner.

3. Sometimes it is difficult to _____ your true feelings.

4. A serious car accident might result in at least one _____.

5. Car manufacturers must _____ with certain safety standards.

6. Because John was angry, he made a _____ attempt to be mean to Paul.

II. *Use the key words from the box to complete the puzzle.*

Down

1. act in agreement with

2. keep in; hold back

3. arouse dislike in

Across

4. intended

5. excessively proud

6. a death

Check your answers with the key on page 55.

The Yellow Rose of Texas

Learn the Key Words

bewitch	(bi wich´)	to fascinate; charm *The adventures of Peter Pan will always* <u>*bewitch*</u> *children.*
famished	(fam´ isht)	to be extremely hungry *The Hearing Dog Training Program has saved many of the stray,* <u>*famished*</u> *dogs on the streets.*
hoodwink	(hu̇d´ wingk)	mislead by a trick; deceive *People complain that some television advertisements try to* <u>*hoodwink*</u> *consumers.*
lust	(lust)	strong desire *American* <u>*lust*</u> *for adventure and success created new frontiers.*
secrete	(si krēt´)	to keep secret; to hide *The squirrel tried to* <u>*secrete*</u> *its supply of food for the winter.*
siesta	(sē es´ tə)	an afternoon nap *In tropical countries, many people take a* <u>*siesta*</u> *after lunch.*

Preview:
1. Read the title.
2. Look at the picture.
3. Read the first four paragraphs of the selection.
4. Then answer the following question.

You learned from your preview that
____a. light rain was falling in Texas.
____b. the "grave" was not for a person, but for the farmers' valuables.
____c. it was an old Mexican custom to bury treasure.
____d. the pine box was loaded with Mexican church crosses.

Turn to the Comprehension Check on page 14 for the right answer.

Now read the selection.

Read to find out about some interesting historical figures.

The Yellow Rose of Texas

Someone you will read about:

Santa Anna (san' tə an' ə) a Mexican general

Places you will read about:

San Jacinto (san jə' sint ō) a county and a river in Texas
The Alamo (al' ə mō) a fort in Texas

The Battle of San Jacinto lasted only eighteen minutes, but it was a decisive victory for the Texans.

It rained continuously for seven days and the temperature had fallen below forty degrees. The strong winds were sweeping the miserable weather across the prairies, flooding the plains, driving men and animals to shelter, but two determined farmers in Texas fought the thick mud with spades and dug a grave.

They dug with frantic motion. Hurrying to complete their work, they dropped the pine box down in the mud pit, covered it, then marked it with a wooden cross.

Their chore accomplished, they ran to the barn where a wagon was loaded with supplies, and an elderly woman sat rigid, clutching three frightened children bundled against the storm. Two servants huddled in the back of the wagon.

There were no tears at the burial, only prayers. They had used the pine box to secrete all their treasures. They prayed that the crude wooden cross would hoodwink the Mexicans when they marched by, raiding the towns and farms that lay in their path.

Late the previous night, their neighbor came fifty miles to warn them that the Alamo had fallen to the Mexicans, and all that was left of the Texas army was retreating with Sam Houston. This was the situation in March 1836.

The women would take the wagon through Indian country to safety in Louisiana, while the men would join Sam Houston and fight for their land.

Sam Houston halted his famished army of volunteers at Groce's plantation. The promise of free land brought these men to Texas, and in their lust for freedom, they declared their independence from Mexico, but had not won it. These rough, reckless volunteers had lost every battle, and the Mexican army had slaughtered almost every man who stood against it.

On April 13th, Sam Houston started his march East. The men grumbled at this retreat, but followed him to Harrisburg, the town where the newly elected "President" of Texas, Burnet, had taken refuge.

Unfortunately, they arrived too late. The town was burned and the President had fled. When they tried to make camp in the slush and mud, they discovered that an epidemic of measles had broken out.

In a rage of anger, Santa Anna burned Harrisburg to the ground when he found that Burnet had escaped him, and continued his pursuit, sending a scout ahead to speed the chase. When the Mexicans finally reached the coast, Burnet had escaped them again by taking a ship to Galveston Island.

Near the shore, the Mexicans found a rich plantation, deserted except for a few of the servants. Santa Anna was furious by now, and he looted and burned the buildings, but the Negroes were permitted to go free. Slavery was against Mexican law, and Santa Anna's war was with white Americans. He even let these Negroes join his camp. One was a girl named Emily. The plantation had belonged to James Morgan, and this girl was one of sixteen Negro servants he had brought with him from North Carolina.

There is a legend in Texas that this girl is the "Yellow Rose," made famous by the popular song, and she is given credit for the

Texan victory, because at just this time in history, Sam Houston's luck began to change.

In April of 1836, James Morgan was in command of Galveston Island which was just across the bay from his plantation. He had with him the Negro servants who knew the network of waterways through the marsh, and could travel quickly from Galveston to the Mexican and Texan camps.

Good fortune fell to Sam Houston the very evening that Emily entered the camp. Sam Houston, with his ailing, half-starved, ill-clad army had just arrived at Harrisburg when the famous Texas spy, Deaf Smith, reported he had just captured a Mexican messenger with three dispatches that revealed the location of two of the Mexican regiments and the exact position of Santa Anna.

Without stopping for rest, Sam Houston lead his tired, but willing, army through the marshes and hid the men in a thicket under an oak grove on the bank of Buffalo Bayou. Before him spread a two mile rising prairie where the two Mexican armies would join together. The cold north wind blew in but the famished men rested, well protected by the aged oaks.

On April 20, Santa Anna arrived and established camp across the field, among the giant oaks. The following morning was warm and full of sunshine and when the second Mexican army arrived, Deaf Smith made his way around the Mexican sentries to count the tent tops, returning to report at least 1500 men. The Texans had less than eight hundred.

Then, Sam Houston had some more luck. For some reason, which was not recorded, during the afternoon of April 21, the Mexican sentries were not on watch. The Texans, in full sunlight, pushed their two cannons across the field of tall grass and opened fire two hundred yards from the Mexican line.

The Battle of San Jacinto lasted eighteen minutes. It was a savage slaughter. The sleeping Mexicans awoke from their siesta in panic to the sudden thunderous cry,

"REMEMBER THE ALAMO!"

It is still a mystery how less than eight hundred rag-tag, starved Texans, defeated a well-armed, strong Mexican army. And how they crossed the prairie without being seen is something else we may never know.

Several years after the battle, James Morgan told a friend that the credit for the victory at San Jacinto belonged to his servant, Emily.

How could Emily bewitch the entire Mexican army long enough for Sam Houston to cross the prairie?

Sam Houston reported that the Texans started at precisely three-thirty in the afternoon, the hour for the Mexicans' siesta. Those men who were not asleep were reported to have been celebrating a feast. The Mexicans believed the war was over and Sam Houston was in retreat. Santa Anna had even tried to make arrangements to return to Mexico by ship. But, why were the Mexican sentries not on watch?

Could Emily have chosen that particular time to hoodwink those men with promises of riches and fortune?

Emily's master was a wealthy man and his plantation was nearby. She could have bewitched them by telling the Mexicans that she would help them find James Morgan's gold, since it was their lust for gold that brought them to Texas in the first place.

In Texas, gold was secreted everywhere, but underground was the only safe place to keep it.

How Emily actually hoodwinked the Mexicans is her secret, and how the Texans overpowered them is amazing. The Texans took as many prisoners as they numbered themselves. It was five days before they could even get word of the victory to the President of Texas on Galveston Island, but James Morgan visited the battlefield two days after the fight.

James Morgan arrived at San Jacinto in a steamship, in time to join the celebration of auctioning the Mexican spoils, where he bid for and purchased Santa Anna's silk tent.

Another mystery about the "Yellow Rose" is her song—no one knows who composed it. The signature on the original handwritten copy in the library at Texas University is only "H.B.C."

It is believed that some of the early lyrics tell of the girl in the song as the "maid of Morgan's Point." If Emily should be among the heroes of San Jacinto, what finer tribute could there be than to have her name forever associated with "The Yellow Rose of Texas."

The Yellow Rose of Texas

COMPREHENSION CHECK

Choose the best answer.

1. The "Yellow Rose of Texas" is said to have been
_____a. James Morgan's mother, Emily.
_____b. James Morgan's servant, Emily.
_____c. Sam Houston's servant, Taylor.
_____d. Sam Houston's wife, Emily.

2. Sam Houston's luck began to change when
_____a. Santa Anna burned Harrisburg.
_____b. Deaf Smith captured a messenger.
_____c. the President escaped from Santa Anna.
_____d. Emily entered Santa Anna's camp.

3. The Texans numbered
_____a. 1500 men.
_____b. about 800 men.
_____c. over 1000 men.
_____d. a few less than the Mexicans.

4. In the battle of San Jacinto, the Texans wanted
_____a. gold.
_____b. revenge.
_____c. Emily.
_____d. land.

5. Emily was
_____a. a frightened, nervous girl.
_____b. a thoughtless, carefree girl.
_____c. one of the first freedom fighters.
_____d. a neglected heroine.

6. This selection might be found in a book called
_____a. "Living in Mexico."
_____b. "A History of Texas."
_____c. "Civil War Heroes."
_____d. "The Revolutionary War."

7. First, Santa Anna made camp across the field from the Texans. Then, the second Mexican army arrived. Next,
_____a. Deaf Smith went to spy on the Mexican sentry.
_____b. the Texans attacked the Mexican camp.
_____c. a wagonload of supplies arrived.
_____d. the Texans pushed cannons onto the field.

8. The Mexicans were not guarding the fort well because they
_____a. thought the Texans were all dead.
_____b. were all sleeping at the same time.
_____c. were all digging for gold.
_____d. thought the war was over.

9. Another name for this selection could be
_____a. "A Dangerous Mission."
_____b. "A War of Nerves."
_____c. "Remember the Alamo!"
_____d. "The Real 'Yellow Rose'."

10. This selection is mainly about
_____a. a young woman who took a chance.
_____b. the events in the battle of the Alamo.
_____c. the turning points in the Texas Revolution.
_____d. slavery as an institution in Texas.

11.   *Develop your own sentences using any four key words found in the box on the following page.*

1. _____
2. _____
3. _____
4. _____

Check your answers with the key on page 53.

The Yellow Rose of Texas

VOCABULARY CHECK

entice	famished	hoodwink	lust	secrete	siesta

I. *Fill in the blank in each sentence with the correct key word from the box above.*

1. After not eating for three days, the dieters were _____.

2. The girl used a nut to _____ the squirrel into coming near.

3. The sharp card player knew he could _____ the others out of a great deal of money.

4. The _____ for excessive power and wealth is a dangerous thing.

5. John decided to _____ his kite among the clothes in his closet so that his little brother would not break it.

6. After his _____, the shopkeeper returned to his store.

II. *Are the following key words used correctly in each sentence? Check yes or no.*

1. If you <u>lust</u> for something, you want it badly.
   _____Yes   _____No

2. To <u>hoodwink</u> someone is to trick them.
   _____Yes   _____No

3. Mother wanted to <u>secrete</u> her new blouse so she left it in full view.
   _____Yes   _____No

4. The candidate tried to <u>entice</u> the people into voting for him by guaranteeing a tax cut.
   _____Yes   _____No

5. If you are <u>famished</u>, you have not eaten anything in an hour.
   _____Yes   _____No

6. Most people take a <u>siesta</u> in the evening.
   _____Yes   _____No

Check your answers with the key on page 56

the Lord of the mountain

Learn the Key Words

aroma (ə rō′ mə) a distinctive fragrance; a pleasant smell
The aroma of the food cooking in the kitchen sharpened his appetite.

captivate (kap′ tə vāt) fascinate; enchant
The actor was able to captivate the audience with his performance.

contemplate (kon′ təm plāt) think about; look at carefully or for a long time
To seek inspiration, artists contemplate the beauty of things around them.

denounce (di nouns′) condemn publicly; express strong disapproval of
The President's opposition tried to denounce him.

disciple (də sī′ pəl) a follower; a strong believer in the thoughts or ways of a leader
The religious leader had many followers, but his most devoted disciple was a man named Paul.

regime (ri zhēm′) the prevailing political or economic system
The Revolution of 1917 established a communist regime in Russia.

Preview:
1. Read the title.
2. Look at the picture.
3. Read the first four paragraphs of the selection.
4. Then answer the following question.

You learned from your preview that
_____a. Ali had deep blue eyes and ebony hair.
_____b. the wine was lacking in taste.
_____c. Ali was being held prisoner in a coffee house.
_____d. Ali was in an unfamiliar surrounding.

Turn to the Comprehension Check on page 19 for the right answer.

Now read the selection.

Read to find out about a little-known historical figure.

the Lord of the mountain

In the eleventh century, one man gained unlimited power in Persia, and controlled the minds of his followers by the use of a mysterious drug.

"Where am I?" Ali wondered, as he awoke feeling somewhat dizzy.

An exquisite face with deep blue eyes and ebony hair came into view.

"Did you sleep well?" the girl asked, while Ali raised a golden bowl of red wine to his mouth and drank the heavily spiced wine to the last drop. The last thing he remembered was accepting a drink in a coffeehouse from a man who congratulated him for winning a music competition, and being invited to perform for the king. He soon became too drowsy to contemplate these matters and was happy to allow this paradise to captivate him.

Later, Ali sat up on the enormous cushion on which he had been sleeping and noticed that he was in a richly decorated tent overlooking a magnificent garden. He noticed, too, that he was no longer in the simple garments of a music student, but in furs and silks fit for a prince. Lovely girls came in to serve him his favorite dishes and more spiced wine, its aroma mingling with the intriguing scent of an herb burning in a bowl.

The beautiful blue-eyed girl began to dance with a rare grace that captivated Ali and reminded him of Yasmin, the little girl who came into his garden to dance whenever he played the flute. Five years ago she had disappeared mysteriously. Ali took the flute from the musician and began to play. The girl danced, looking more and more like Yasmin.

When she bowed at his feet, he whispered to her, "Yasmin? It is I, Ali."

She searched his face for a long moment, tears welling up in her eyes.

"Look for me near the fountain tonight," she said, and ran out of the tent.

"The Lord of the Mountain will see you in the castle," another girl told Ali, then disappeared before he could ask who the Lord was. Questions and doubt evaporated from his mind as he stepped into the garden. Rainbow-colored flowers carpeted the field before him, their delightful perfume fanned toward him by a soft breeze. Fruits and nuts hung temptingly from the trees, on whose branches song birds were giving a concert to an audience of deer, peacocks and a tiger. The delicious spiced wine gushed out of a fountain nearby.

"This must be Paradise," Ali thought as he quenched his thirst and felt as if he were walking on air.

The white castle floated on the middle of a lake full of swans. Ali was rowed across on a flower-decked boat to the silver gates and was led into a hall filled with the aroma of a strange herb burning in golden bowls. Inside, a bearded man in a white mantle sat on an ivory throne.

"I am the Lord of the Mountain and I welcome you to Paradise, my son," he said. "I hope you are happy here."

Ali replied, "Heaven is better than what my grandfather said it would be. Are my father and grandfather here, too?"

"Well," said the Lord, clearing his throat, "you will see them, but not until you have proved yourself worthy to stay here forever."

Ali looked questioningly at him.

"We brought you here temporarily," the Lord explained, "in order to give you a taste of Paradise so that you will have the courage to do the great deed for which you are destined as my disciple."

"I do not understand," Ali said quietly.

"As the winner of the music competition," the Lord continued, "you will perform for the king in his palace. When everybody is lulled by your music, you will stab the king with a poisoned dagger. You will be executed for your crime, but will come straight back to live eternally in Paradise."

"Murder the king!" Ali exclaimed in disbelief.

"Yes," the Lord replied, "his regime keeps Persia from progressing. Besides, he murdered your father and blamed bandits for the crime. It is your duty to denounce the king and avenge your father's death."

Astounded and confused, Ali remained silent.

"I realize that you require time to contemplate this matter," the Lord continued, "but before you return to the garden, I want you to witness something."

The Lord clapped his hands and a guard brought in an apparently hypnotized young man who knelt before the Lord while an executioner proceeded to chop off the youth's head. The Lord covered the headless body with his mantle and as his disciples chanted to the beating of the drums, the deceased man sprang out of the mantle, alive, with a new head on his shoulders. He picked up his old, bleeding head from the carpet and tossed it on Ali's lap, shouting, "I have returned from death to live forever in Paradise."

Ali fainted.

When he regained consciousness, the moon was high in the sky and Yasmin was wiping his forehead with a cool towel.

"Back in Paradise, at last," he sighed.

"We are not in Paradise," Yasmin said sadly. "I was kidnapped by bandits and sold to the Lord as a slave," she explained, "and you were drugged at the coffeehouse and brought here by his disciples. The wine you have been drinking contains a rare drug, *hashish*, a plant known only to the Lord. The burning herb whose smoke you inhaled, was the same. It kept you dreaming even while you were awake. The Lord gives hashish to his disciples to make them believe that they are in Paradise. That is why they are called Hashishins."

"Is the tiger in the garden drugged too?" Ali asked.

"Yes," she replied, "and he is old and toothless, too."

"What about the dead man who came back to life?" Ali asked.

"One disciple," she explained, "accepted the execution believing that he would dwell in Paradise forever. Another man came out of a trap door to replace the corpse. If you were not drugged, you would have seen through the trick. Your father was killed in a similar ceremony for refusing to cooperate with the Lord against the king's regime."

"I am going to destroy that monster," declared Ali.

"Only his most trusted disciples can approach him," Yasmin said.

"We will escape and bring back soldiers," he insisted.

Yasmin led him to the stone wall surrounding the garden. The garden was perched on a high cliff, surrounded on one side by a deep gorge, and on the other by a deep valley which was heavily guarded by the Lord's disciples and vicious dogs. She advised Ali to pretend to go along with the Lord's orders and denounce him only when safe in the king's protection. He wanted to smuggle her out in a sack, but Yasmin sadly told him that the guards searched everything and if they were caught, they would be executed. She would stay behind and warn others who were unfortunate enough to be lured there.

On the day of Ali's departure from "Paradise," Yasmin asked him to deliver her bracelet to her mother.

"Please tell her that I am well," she murmured, embracing Ali, "and remember me when you play the flute."

"I'll come back for you," he whispered in her ear before an impatient guard blindfolded him securely and strapped him on a donkey that would carry him back to his home.

Ali never found his way back to the Hashishin fortress. Every night, when the moon rose over the garden, he played his flute for Yasmin, who danced in the garden which imprisoned her to the end of her days. The Lord of the Mountain and his heirs continued to rule this way for two hundred years more until the Mongol invaders from the North found their secret garden and destroyed it. His followers, Hashishins, were later called "assassins," and the name eventually came to mean "one who murders for a political cause."

the LORD of the mountain

COMPREHENSION CHECK

Choose the best answer.

1. The Lord of the Mountain
____a. ruled with logic and good sense.
____b. had few disciples in his community.
____c. ruled with a secret drug.
____d. used no force or violence.

2. The people in the mountain community were
____a. manipulated and deceived.
____b. free to leave at any time.
____c. fully aware of their commitment.
____d. interested in the future of Persia.

3. Before he was abducted, Ali was
____a. unsure of himself and his lifestyle.
____b. searching for his father.
____c. unhappy as a musician.
____d. secure and settled in his beliefs.

4. The task assigned to Ali by the Lord of the Mountain was to
____a. rule Persia.
____b. kill the king.
____c. direct the community.
____d. lead Yasmin out of captivity.

5. The Lord of the Mountain was
____a. a sick and power-hungry creature.
____b. a merciful and loving leader.
____c. a supporter of the king.
____d. sincere about his way of life.

6. If Ali had not met Yasmin, he probably would
____a. have returned home, unharmed.
____b. have continued with his music.
____c. never have realized the truth of his situation.
____d. have become one of the leaders in the cult.

7. First, Ali was drugged in a coffeehouse. Then, he awakened in a richly embroidered tent. Next,
____a. he was put on a donkey and blindfolded.
____b. he recognized an old friend named Yasmin.
____c. he attempted to kill the Lord of the Mountain.
____d. he waited for Yasmin to return to his garden.

8. The rule of the Lord of the Mountain and his followers was ended by the
____a. king.
____b. Mongols.
____c. captives.
____d. musician.

9. Another name for this selection could be
____a. "An Illusion of Paradise."
____b. "Life in Persia."
____c. "A Musician's Dream."
____d. "A Place to Escape."

10. This selection is mainly about
____a. a beautiful garden in Persia.
____b. the devious tactics of a madman.
____c. an unusual, but fulfilling way of life.
____d. a community in which cooperation is vital.

11. *Develop your own sentences using any four key words found in the box on the following page.*

1 _____

2 _____

3 _____

4 _____

Check your answers with the key on page 53.

This page may be reproduced for classroom use.

the lord of the mountain

aroma	captivate	contemplate	denounce	disciple	regime

VOCABULARY CHECK

I.   Fill in the blank in each sentence with the correct key word from the box above.

1. The woman could _____ a room full of people with her dazzling smile.

2. Hitler's _____ brought terror and defeat to the people of Germany.

3. The _____ of freshly baked bread spread throughout the house.

4. The statesman will _____ the use of drugs to control and detain any person.

5. Before making a decision, a person should _____ all choices and possibilities.

6. As a _____ , a person must trust the one he or she follows.

II.   Use the key words to fill in the blanks in the puzzle.

Across

1. think about carefully

3. a follower or believer

5. a form of government

Down

1. fascinate or enchant

2. a distinct smell or flavor

4. accuse or condemn

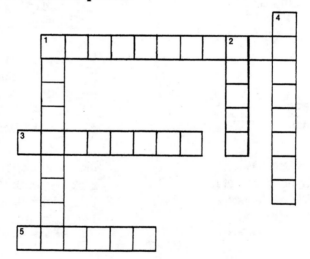

Check your answers with the key on page 56.

The End of Eden

Learn the Key Words

compress   (kəm pres′)   squeeze together; make smaller by pressure
A trash compactor is used to compress garbage.

consecutive   (kən sek′ yə tiv)   successive; following without interruption
The days of the week follow in consecutive order.

disrupt   (dis rupt′)   break apart; shatter
The Civil War served to disrupt the harmony of the United States.

prism   (priz′ əm)   a transparent solid figure, usually glass, used for separating beams of light
When holding the prism up to the sun, Jackie could see a rainbow of colors.

propel   (prə pel′)   drive or push forward; force ahead
You propel a boat with oars.

serene   (sə rēn′)   peaceful; calm
The atmosphere in the garden was relaxed and serene.

Preview:
1. Read the title.
2. Look at the picture.
3. Read the first two paragraphs of the selection.
4. Then answer the following question.

You learned from your preview that
_____a. Sais was a professional musician during the Middle Ages.
_____b. the story occurs in the middle of the summer.
_____c. Sais enjoyed the Middle Ages for its serenity.
_____d. Sais and her husband, Elkin, were from the Orient.

Turn to the Comprehension Check on page 24 for the right answer.

Now read the selection.

Read to find out what happens when history is changed.

The End of Eden

What would happen if we could travel through time as easily as traveling to another country, and the smallest change in events could alter the course of history dramatically?

The merchants' tents formed a tapestry of color and activity against the serene hillside, and wandering minstrels delighted everyone with their music. A spring breeze wove its way through the booths of proudly exhibited goods. Touching lightly upon Flemish wools and Spanish leathers, it gently swirled the cloaks of strolling people, and then finally gathering more strength, it rippled the colorful silks displayed by jeweled traders from the Orient.

Sais put down her flute and leaned against the tree to take in the lively atmosphere of the fair. The fair, to which people came from every part of the country to take delight in each other's accomplishments, was one of the reasons she and her husband, Elkin, enjoyed vacationing in the Middle Ages. Of course they always liked the excitement of the first space launchings in the 20th Century, or the celebrations in honor of the galactic ambassador's arrival in the 21st, but the quiet gracefulness of the Middle Ages seemed unique. Yes, thought Sais, next vacation they would

return here.

A sound of drums and the single blare of a horn served to disrupt Sais from her daydreams. Cupping her hand to her forehead, she saw across the field a bouquet of colored banners fluttering against the bright sky. It was the procession of townspeople, acrobats and children. Elkin, who had spent time in the village performing with the other minstrels, would surely be among them.

As the procession reached the center of the fairground, the minstrels broke into song, and the acrobats, dressed in crimson and gold, tumbled forward and quickly flipped over backwards in a series of consecutive movements, to the delight of the children who clumsily tried to mimic their movements. A number of people, enthused by the music, joined hands and danced in a circle around the bouncing acrobats. One of the minstrels strummed his lute in a final sweeping gesture, took a long deep bow, and began threading his way through the crowd toward one of the sprawling oak trees that

hemmed the fair.

Waiting for Elkin by the trees, Sais looked to the west and saw that the setting sun had become a huge orange ball that seemed delicately balanced on the hilltop. She instinctively reached into her pocket and clutched the tiny prism, wondering what could be keeping Elkin.

"Sais, I've been looking for you!" Elkin greeted her with a wide grin, as he walked toward her with a jaunty gait.

It was hard to be angry with him, even if he was always late and did seem a bit careless at times.

"It's time to leave, Elkin." Sais touched his arm and turned toward the sunset. "We'll just be able to catch the last rays of sunlight."

Sais and Elkin hurried to the forest, where the festive music and laughter dissolved into the haunting silence of the trees, and cobwebs of shadows were being cast along the ground by the sun's last orange rays winking amid the dense foliage. Only the rustle of a squirrel disrupted the stillness as Sais withdrew the prism from her pocket, and held it up to the sky.

The prism began to glow with a brilliant white light that seemed to compress all of the remaining daylight. A soft whistling sound, like wind blowing through a cave, suddenly filled the forest. The area of light around the prism began giving off ripples of rainbow colors. The whistling sound rose to a high pitch as the colors expanded to enfold Sais and Elkin who then disappeared.

The squirrel that had been perched perfectly motionless on a branch overhead, flicked his puffed tail and quickly scampered down the tree. The forest was dark now.

Sais and Elkin stood by the window of their living dome which overlooked a peaceful city of arched buildings and spiraling sky roadways. Gleaming space taxis, arriving from various parts of the galaxy, glided serenely by as if they were being carried by the current of an invisible stream. The Fulfillment Age, the sum total of a human history that never knew war or poverty, spread before them like an abundant feast. It was a truly magnificent sight.

"I saw something interesting today." Elkin paused as he slowly stirred his coffee. Then, quickly tapping the spoon on the rim of the cup, he continued. "It's that old prism in the museum."

"Don't tell me you believe in that story about the existence of a forbidden time?" Sais said as she turned from the window.

"Why not?" Elkin put his cup down firmly. "Why would the one thing forbidden by the world government be the removal of that prism if such a time didn't exist?"

There were many stories about the old prism, one of the first ever made. Supposedly, it was magical and no one could stare at it. It was also said that the prism would propel the traveler to a time even greater than the present and the traveler would not wish to return. But above all else, everyone knew that it was forbidden to touch.

In the weeks that followed, Sais and Elkin talked more and more about the prism. It became a fundamental part of their lives and it was with them like a third person. Even in silence they could read it in each other's mind.

Finally, one day, the news spread through the city like a quiver: the old time prism was missing.

When the colors faded and the whistling sounds ceased, Sais and Elkin found themselves in a lush garden at daybreak. As the slit of light on the horizon widened, the garden became transformed. The flower buds opened like spreading fans and the fruit on the trees ripened before their very eyes. Elkin picked an apple and took a big bite.

"You see," he said to Sais, "I knew it would work. This can be our own private time to come back..."

He was suddenly interrupted by the appearance of a beautiful woman, who was staring at the apple in his hand. Elkin shrugged his shoulders.

"Here," he said, extending the fruit to her. "It's delicious."

The woman hesitated, then took the apple and bit into it.

"Eve!"

Sais and Elkin turned to see a man standing behind them, his face frozen in horror.

The woman smiled sweetly and said, "You see, Adam, these fruits are not poisonous at all."

Propelled by a sudden thrust, Sais and Elkin saw consecutive periods of history flash by, like the scenery from a speeding locomotive, as thousands of years were being compressed in an instant. When the brilliant lights faded and the roaring sounds halted, they found themselves at the perimeter of a forest. The day was grey and cold and toward the hillside they could see a cluster of tents being blown by a fierce wind.

"It's the fair, I'm certain of it," Sais shouted, "but something is different."

Off to one side, a long procession of hooded figures slowly entered the fairground and wound through the booths, like serpents, chanting, "Repent!" "Repent!" People fell to their knees and some, whose clothes were torn and tattered, held out their hands to the hooded figures. Then another procession rode by. This time the figures were horsemen wearing polished black armor and long silver blades hung at their sides. The people cleared a path for them, and cowered in fear.

Sais and Elkin began to fear what they had done and what they would find in their own time.

The End of Eden

COMPREHENSION CHECK

Choose the best answer.

1. In Sais and Elkin's day
____a. time travel was accepted and enjoyed.
____b. the world was in a terrible state.
____c. there was no government or laws.
____d. the people were displeased with life.

2. Sais and Elkin were
____a. satisfied and happy.
____b. adventurous and reckless.
____c. miserable and envious.
____d. respectable and obedient.

3. The human race had reached the Fulfillment Age
____a. after years of struggling.
____b. with little strife or trouble.
____c. because of Sais and Elkin.
____d. by using the old time prism.

4. Using the old time prism from the museum, the couple went back in time to
____a. the twentieth century.
____b. the Garden of Eden.
____c. prehistoric times.
____d. the country of their choice.

5. The author of this story
____a. weaves certain known facts into a fictional work.
____b. is relating a true story based on historical fact.
____c. presents the reader with an unknown biography.
____d. possesses some special information unknown to most.

6. According to the selection, Sais and Elkin
____a. went unnoticed in a new time.
____b. affected nothing by their adventure.
____c. lead the way for others to use the old prism.
____d. changed the course of history.

7. First, Sais and Elkin went back in time to the Middle Ages. Then, they returned to their own time. Next,
____a. they appeared in what seemed to be a paradise.
____b. they went on a vacation to a future time.
____c. they concentrated on the forbidden prism.
____d. they danced at the fair.

8. In a certain sense, Sais and Elkin
____a. made a good decision to steal the old prism.
____b. were the Adam and Eve of the Fulfillment Age.
____c. belonged to the Middle Ages.
____d. changed the world for the better.

9. Another name for this selection could be
____a. "The Forbidden Time."
____b. "A Time for Adventure."
____c. "Peace in Another Time."
____d. "Exciting Vacations."

10. This selection is mainly about
____a. time travel in the 20th century.
____b. the direct effect of one's actions on others.
____c. how people lived in the Middle Ages.
____d. the beginning of the world as we know it.

11. *Develop your own sentences using any four key words found in the box on the following page.*

1 _____

2 _____

3 _____

4 _____

Check your answers with the key on page 53.

The End of Eden

VOCABULARY CHECK

compress	consecutive	disrupt	prism	propel	serene

I. *Fill in the blank in each sentence with the correct key word from the box above.*

1. Our cabin was set on a _____ hilltop, which overlooked the lake.

2. After four _____ home runs, the player was under tremendous pressure from his fans to hit another.

3. The couple left the young child at home with the baby-sitter because they believed that he might _____ the party.

4. Kicking one's feet will _____ one through the water.

5. Factories _____ certain types of wood to make a kind of building board.

6. A _____ reflects light in many different colors.

II. *Match the key words in Column A with the definitions in Column B.*

Column A	Column B
____1. compress	a. successive
____2. prism	b. shatter
____3. propel	c. squeeze together
____4. disrupt	d. a transparent solid figure
____5. serene	e. drive or push forward
____6. consecutive	f. peaceful; calm

Check your answers with the key on page 57.

RACE THE CHUCKWAGONS

Learn the Key Words

coordination   (kō ôrd n ā′ shən)   working together; in proper order
The four-horse team worked with perfect <u>coordination</u>.

dejected   (di jek′ tid)   in low spirits
Mary was <u>dejected</u> when the trip was cancelled.

disqualify   (dis kwol′ ə fī)   declare unfit or unable to do something
When the cowboy fell off the horse, the judges had to <u>disqualify</u> the team.

lament   (lə ment′)   express grief; mourn
David thought it was foolish to <u>lament</u> his bad luck.

stress   (stres)   great pressure; strain
They were working under great <u>stress</u>.

wistful   (wist′ fəl)   longing; showing a desire for
He looked at the prize with <u>wistful</u> eyes.

Preview:

1. Read the title.
2. Look at the picture.
3. Read the first three paragraphs of the selection.
4. Then answer the following question.

You learned from your preview that
_____a. the entire story takes place in Cheyenne, Wyoming.
_____b. Dick Pendleton owned the Prime Time restaurant.
_____c. Dick was enthusiastic about describing the Frontier Days.
_____d. Dick's specialty was racing on the Midway.

Turn to the Comprehension Check on page 29 for the right answer.

Now read the selection.

Read to find out about a modern frontier.

RACE THE CHUCKWAGONS

The key to racing chuckwagons was skill and coordination. Could Denny do it?

"Cheyenne, Wyoming, that's the place. The daddy of all the 'Frontier Days'," said old Dick Pendleton with a wistful sigh.

The weatherbeaten old horse trainer was a thin little man with a large high-boned nose and a yellowing droopy fringe of a moustache. He was also the only customer in Art White's Prime Time restaurant that wintery evening in Alberta, Canada. Unable to get back to his ranch because of the bad weather and not particularly anxious to retire to his hotel room, Dick had Art's son, Denny, and the other waiter, Harold Moon, spellbound at his yarns, as they all hunched over a table, devouring steak and listening to the howling wind outside.

"Yep," added Dick, "racing chuckwagons, that's my specialty. They assign you a cart with a tarpaulin on top, where you print your sponsor's name. The carts all measure ten feet long. Attached to the back is a feedbox. You've got to guide your four-horse team around these here four barrels," Dick moved a spoon around a cluster of salt and pepper shakers, "and our outriders, that's two men

on horseback riding alongside, have to take a black box they call the 'stove' and throw it into your feedbox while you're in motion. Then the whole contraption goes racing around the track. They figure the winner on points, not only for coming in first. They disqualify you for knocking down a barrel or not getting the 'stove' in the feedbox, or if one of the outriders isn't with the chuckwagon at the end of the race. And you should see that Midway—music and lights and rides. Yep, that was some town during the Frontier Days."

He looked innocently up at the ceiling.

"$5,000 purse for a night's work. They let you race twice during the week; that's $10,000 if you win twice. I've never lost a chuckwagon race yet. Wish I had two good outriders and a sponsor. I'd tackle those chuckwagon races again this summer. I can just see that $10,000 check, so pretty and green."

This last wistful remark was for Art White's benefit.

Art's eyes flickered, ever so slightly, toward the worn out

paneling on the side wall of the restaurant and the broken tiles on the floor. $5,000 could go a long way toward sprucing the place up.

Suddenly, Art slapped his hand down on the table.

"All right," he told Dick, "I'll sponsor you for half of the purse. I'll give the boys time off to be your outriders."

The $10,000 purse didn't turn out to be two nights' work, as Dick had advertised. It was more like a whole winter when the weather was decent, and the entire spring into the middle of July, of hard work for Denny and Harold out at Dick's ranch. Dick had a four-horse team of powerful black thoroughbreds that moved like locomotives. He had rigged up a cart exactly like the ones used at Cheyenne and he trained his team to pull the cart around four barrels without knocking any over, while Denny and Harold, at full gallop, practiced throwing a 'stove' box into the feedbox at the rear of the cart. Then, with Dick yelling, "Stay close! Don't lose the wagon," they all went, four-horse team neighing and snorting, the ramshackle wagon with the whooping old man and the two outriders dashing to keep up, tearing around the field, a masterpiece of coordination.

They finally left for Wyoming in the middle of July in Art's camper with the horses in a trailer. Cheyenne was hot and crowded with tourists who had come for the Frontier Days and Denny and Harold took in the Midway, when they weren't watching the rodeo. But, best of all was the parade, where all the participants in the events rode through the streets of Cheyenne. Wearing his green vest, coordinated with the green lettering on the Prime Time wagon, Denny sat proudly atop Spitfire. He and that stallion were like a machine, working with perfect coordination. Denny had raised the horse from a colt and had cared for and trained him.

That evening, as the Wyoming sky faded from deep blue to dark grey and the Prime Time team moved into place for the chuckwagon race, Denny leaned over his horse's mane and whispered to Spitfire, "We're going to win that $5,000 tonight—one half for Pa to fix up the restaurant."

"Go!" shouted the starter.

The race proceeded like a dream. The Prime Time wagon thundered out onto the track way ahead of the other wagons. They were going down the straightaway, Denny and Harold keeping close behind Dick, when suddenly the stadium lights flashed on. Spitfire uttered a loud "neigh" and reared up on his hind legs.

"Steady boy!" shouted Denny, frantically pulling on the reins, but the stallion was already out of control. He careened off the track, back towards the barrels, and with one last wailing lament, dumped Denny off his back.

More embarrassed than hurt by the calamity, Denny finally got Spitfire to calm down, but the Prime Time team, in spite of coming in first, was disqualified because both outriders were not with the wagon at the finish. Slowly, Denny led his horse back to the trailer and wiped him down. Then, walking over to the back of the camper, he crouched in the dark, thoroughly dejected.

Wistfully, he listened to the loud laughter coming from the cowboys at the encampment next door. The other people's good time just made him feel more miserable. He lost the race and half of the $5,000 that was supposed to help his father, and all because he let himself be thrown like a six year old just learning to ride.

Recognizing Dick's firm footsteps crunching on the gravel walk, Denny hung his head in an even more dejected pose. The old man would feel sorry for him and say a comforting word. Denny needed that.

But Dick just stood there, his moustache drooping with disgust.

"A little bit of stress and you fall apart. And now you're playing the big 'poor me' game. What a waste of time you are!"

"It wasn't my fault," Denny nearly cried. "Spitfire was frightened by the lights."

"So do something about it instead of just sitting there," snorted Dick, heading toward the Indian tents.

A flash of rage came and went in Denny, leaving a new thought. How stupid to waste the time by being dejected. The horse had to become accustomed to the lights.

He saddled up Spitfire again and rode him towards the spotlights, over and over again, gentling him down every time he reared. The next day, Harold and Dick used flashlights to get the stallion used to sudden light.

As the time for the chuckwagon race approached the next night, Denny talked to the horse lovingly, smoothing its neck with slow strokes. The starter shouted "Go!" and Prime Time went faultlessly through its paces again. The lights flashed and Spitfire reared, but Denny kept him going.

The team was racing around the track heading for the finish line, when the sound of hoofbeats came up close behind. Then the Ace Hardware wagon rattled past Denny, nearly knocking him to the ground. Up ahead, Dick urged his thoroughbreds on, while Ace kept pushing the Prime Time cart to the side, trying to edge the wagon off the track.

"Ayeow!" yelled Dick, slashing his whip. The Prime Time thoroughbreds with nostrils flaring and black manes flying, charged ahead of Ace Hardware,

while Denny and Harold galloped on either side of the wagon until it flashed across the finish line.

The Prime Time team high-stepped proudly down the track encouraged by the thrilling shouts of an enthusiastic crowd and Denny felt his horse move under him, charged with the excitement. Then when Dick accepted the prize money with a funny little old-fashioned bow, Denny realized that he was bringing home more than the prize money for his father. He had learned something important; that when there's stress, you don't stop to lament over your problems, but you just figure out what to do and keep on moving!

RACE THE CHUCKWAGONS

COMPREHENSION CHECK

Preview Answer:

c. Dick was enthusiastic about describing the Frontier Days.

Choose the best answer.

1. A chuckwagon is a
____a. ten-foot long cart with a tarpaulin on top.
____b. wagon that contains an enormous amount of food.
____c. new type of camper with kitchen facilities.
____d. small animal that eats only wood shavings.

2. Denny
____a. was a selfish young riding star.
____b. lost the first race on purpose.
____c. wanted to enter a contest alone.
____d. loved his father very much.

3. If Denny had not entered the chuckwagon race, he
____a. would have been a successful show rider.
____b. might never have learned how to bear up under pressure.
____c. would have done the improvements on his father's place.
____d. would have been unhappy living in Alaska.

4. The chuckwagon races were
____a. part of a fair called Frontier Days in Cheyenne, Wyoming.
____b. a tradition begun by the cooks in the pioneer days.
____c. just friendly competition between local Alaskans.
____d. directed by the Indians in the Cheyenne area.

5. First, the Prime Time team lost the race when Spitfire reared and Denny was thrown off. Then, Dick reprimanded Denny for sulking and giving up. Next,
____a. Denny packed his things and rode Spitfire home alone.
____b. Denny entered a team with the Ace Hardware team.
____c. Denny tried to get Spitfire used to the stadium lights.
____d. Denny and the Prime Time team won the race.

6. According to the selection, which of the following rules is *not* used for gaining points in a chuckwagon race?
____a. Coming in first with the best time
____b. One outrider finishing with the wagon
____c. Not knocking over any barrels
____d. Getting the "stove" inside the feedbox

7. Art White sponsored the Prime Time wagon because he
____a. wanted to call Dick's bluff as a racer.
____b. wanted his son to be a famous chuckwagon star.
____c. needed the prize money for repairs in his business.
____d. wanted the money to take a vacation in Wyoming.

8. Dick was
____a. an incompetent rancher.
____b. a clever horse trainer.
____c. a bitter old man.
____d. a patient person.

9. Another name for this selection could be
____a. "Boxcar Races."
____b. "Wyoming Winds."
____c. "Alaskan Winters."
____d. "A Prime Time to Win."

10. This selection is mainly about
____a. fighting to keep a business alive in Alaska.
____b. learning to prepare for and see something through.
____c. the days of the old wild west in Wyoming.
____d. a father who burdens his only son.

11.   *Develop your own sentences using any four key words found in the box on the following page.*

1. _____
2. _____
3. _____
4. _____

Check your answers with the key on page 53.

RACE THE CHUCKWAGONS

VOCABULARY CHECK

| coordination | dejected | disqualify | lament | stress | wistful |

I.   Fill in the blank in each sentence with the correct key word from the box above.

1.   The _____ of the group was essential for a united effort.

2.   Paul was _____ after he was rejected from the college of choice.

3.   The officials had to _____ the player because of his unsportsmanlike conduct.

4.   Too much _____ can make one nervous or short-tempered.

5.   No one can tell you not to _____ over the loss of a loved one.

6.   As the little boy stared at the candy sticks, a _____ expression came across his tiny face.

II.   Choose the correct key word that could replace the underlined words.

1.   We will have to reject anyone who cheats.
   ____a. dejected   ____c. lament
   ____b. stress   ____d. disqualify
2.   It is important to emphasize all of his good points.
   ____a. disqualify   ____c. stress
   ____b. lament   ____d. wistful
3.   The team's great working together helped them defeat their opponents.
   ____a. coordination   ____c. lament
   ____b. stress   ____d. dejected
4.   He stared into the night, full of longing desires.
   ____a. dejected   ____c. disqualified
   ____b. wistful   ____d. coordinating
5.   John knew Paula would mourn the death of her dog.
   ____a. disqualify   ____c. lament
   ____b. stress   ____d. wistful
6.   Kevin was in low spirits after he failed his test.
   ____a. dejected   ____c. coordinated
   ____b. wistful   ____d. stress

Check your answers with the key on page 57.

FIRST AND FOREMOST

Learn the Key Words

audition	(ô dish ′ ən)	a trial performance to test the abilities of a performer *Mary decided to <u>audition</u> for the musical because she likes to sing.*
champagne	(sham pān ′)	a bubbly wine *The bride and groom poured <u>champagne</u> for the wedding guests.*
diction	(dik ′ shən)	one's manner of speaking with regard to clearness or effectiveness *Her <u>diction</u> was so poor that no one could understand what she was saying.*
disapprove	(dis ə prüv ′)	show dislike; express an opinion against *Ellen thought her mother would <u>disapprove</u> of her new hairdo.*
encore	(än ′ kôr)	an extra performance by a performer after entertainment has ended *At the end of the play, the audience would not stop clapping until the star returned for an <u>encore</u>.*
undertone	(un ′ dər tōn)	something spoken in a quiet manner *"I didn't do my homework," John told his friend in an <u>undertone</u>, as the teacher passed out a test.*

Preview:
1. Read the title.
2. Look at the picture.
3. Read the first three paragraphs of the selection.
4. Then answer the following question.

You learned from your preview that
____a. Anna Cora always dreamed of becoming an actress.
____b. in the 19th century, acting was not considered a respectable career.
____c. many people attended the theater in 1819.
____d. Anna Cora began her acting career when she was nine.

Turn to the Comprehension Check on page 34 for the right answer.

Now read the selection.

Read to find out about a very resourceful and gifted woman.

FIRST AND FOREMOST

Early in the nineteenth century, a very talented woman proved that the best place for women is not always in the home.

Anna Cora Mowatt was a famous actress of the nineteenth century and the first American woman to write a successful play.

Today, most people enjoy the theater and have respect for actors and actresses, but, in 1819 when Anna Cora was born, the theater had a poor reputation. Acting was not an honorable profession. Auditoriums were neither clean nor comfortable, and audiences were noisy and rude. Many Americans refused to attend the theater. On the other hand, reading plays in books was a popular pastime. So, although many people were familiar with published plays, few had seen these productions on a stage.

Anna Cora was the ninth child in a family of eleven. Her father was a successful businessman, and her mother was well educated. As a child, Anna enjoyed creating games for her brothers and sisters. Sometimes, they would present scenes from famous plays on a wooden platform in the backyard for an audience of two—their parents.

Because the theater itself was not considered an appropriate career for a person from a good family, she never thought about becoming an actress herself.

When Anna was fifteen, a young man named James Mowatt began visiting the large household. He was a lawyer from a respected New York family, who was looking for a wife. At first, he courted one of Anna Cora's older sisters, but then he met Anna Cora.

"From the first moment I saw you," James later explained, "you managed to captivate me with your sunny personality and your joy for living."

Soon, James was talking about marriage. Anna Cora finally agreed to elope with him, more because she was thrilled at the prospect of an adventure than because she actually loved him. However, she soon came to care deeply about her new husband.

"Since you married me before you finished school, I think it would be a good idea for you to spend part of each day reading books," James told her. "In that way, you'll be able to complete your education here at home." Anna Cora agreed and even tried writing poetry, with James' encouragement.

A few months later, Anna Cora developed a lung ailment that required treatment in Europe. While she was there, she wrote articles for American magazines about her impressions of life abroad. When she returned home, she discovered that James had invested most of their money foolishly, and they were almost broke. On top of that, James became ill and couldn't continue in his law practice. "I must do something to support my husband and myself," she realized, "but what exactly can I do?"

A few days later, she had an idea. "When I was younger," she told James, "my sisters and brothers and I used to give dramatic readings for our family. I thoroughly enjoyed that, and I believe I was rather good. Our parents often praised my clear diction, which made it possible to understand every word I spoke. I'll give a series of readings from plays and other works of literature."

In the 1840's, it was very rare to see a woman appearing as a public personality, so many of the people who attended Anna Cora's early performances were there out of curiosity. However, nearly everyone was captivated by her, and she became very popular. On several occasions, her audiences were not content to leave at the end of the regular program of readings, and Anna Cora would be asked to give an encore.

One evening she was dining in a restaurant with friends after a performance, when two well-dressed strangers approached the table.

"The taller gentleman is Mr. Barry, who manages a theater," someone whispered in an undertone to her.

"Mrs. Mowatt, I must tell you how very much I enjoyed your readings this evening," Mr. Barry began. "I wonder if you know what a triumph it would be if you appeared on the stage as an actress?"

"I appreciate your kind words, sir," Anna Cora replied, "but I cannot imagine myself in that situation."

A waiter hurried to the table carrying a bottle of champagne and several wine glasses.

"At least permit me to offer a toast to your continued good fortune," Mr. Barry said, reaching for a glass of champagne which the waiter poured. "I will leave you to your guests," he added, "but if you should change your mind, I hope you will come to audition for me."

As Mr. Barry walked away, Anna Cora was blinking in surprise. "Imagine me as an actress!" she laughed.

Her readings earned money, but the Mowatts still had debts, so Anna Cora returned to the activity of writing magazine articles. As she did, she remembered Mr. Barry's remark that she had talent for the theater. "I wonder," she said to James, "if I could write a comedy for the stage?"

"You'll only be able to answer that question if you try it," was his encouraging answer.

Anna Cora had mixed feelings. She thought that people would disapprove of the idea. She knew that certain plays from England were respected by Americans, although those from her own country were still looked down upon. "Why shouldn't an American be able to write a good play, too?" she thought. And yet, Anna Cora feared she might disgrace herself by writing for the theater, a form of entertainment that most of her friends considered unimportant, and disapproved of.

"I don't care," she finally decided. "James is right, and I will try it!"

In less than two months, Anna Cora wrote a comedy about a scoundrel from Europe who hopes to fool a family of Americans into giving him all their money, until he is exposed by an honest American farmer. The play also poked fun at people who believe that anything from Europe must automatically be good. She called her comedy *Fashion*. When the manager of the Park Theater in New York read it, he was captivated and immediately scheduled it for his 1845 season of plays.

The opening of *Fashion* was an event in New York society. Mrs. Mowatt's name helped to make the performance respectable, and a good many people who attended were coming to a theater for the first time in their lives.

Fashion was extremely popular both with audiences and with drama critics. One of the play's most ardent supporters was Edgar Allan Poe, who later became famous for his many short stories of horror and imagination. In 1845, Poe was a reporter in New York, assigned to cover the theater. "*Fashion* is superior to any other American play!" he wrote.

With the success of her play, Anna Cora was approached by the manager of the Park Theater and the theater's leading actor, Mr. Crisp. They hoped to persuade her to become an actress.

"I believe you only make this offer to me because I am a curiosity—a woman who has written a play," she replied to them.

"On the contrary! Your diction is perfect, your posture is beautiful, and you have a charming manner that will captivate everyone," Mr. Crisp told her. "You may select any role you choose, and there is no need to audition for it. The part is yours."

"I'm certain they are sincere," James told Anna Cora in an undertone.

"Then I will do it!" she exclaimed suddenly. "If you all believe in me, and if I believe in myself, how can I fail?"

Anna Cora appeared first in *The Lady of Lyons*, a drama, and was an instant success. Every night the audience applauded wildly until she returned for an encore. After this triumph, Anna Cora starred in more than two dozen comedies and dramas, each more popular than the last. Her greatest achievement was to appear on the stage in Europe, where she was acclaimed as the best American actress of her generation. At the time of her death in 1870, Anna Cora Mowatt had proven beyond all doubt that a woman could be a successful writer, and that the theater could be enjoyed by people from all backgrounds.

Mrs. Mowatt recorded the events of her extraordinary life in her charming *Autobiography of an Actress*, published in 1853.

FIRST AND FOREMOST

COMPREHENSION CHECK

Choose the best answer.

Preview Answer:
b. in the 19th century, acting was not considered a respectable career.

(1.) Anna Cora Mowatt was
_____a. an actress with expensive tastes.
_____b. a woman who was far behind her times.
_____c. a woman with insight and charm.
_____d. an interesting, but unsuccessful figure.

2. *Fashion* was a
_____a. comedy with social implications, written by Anna Cora.
_____b. drama that starred Anna Cora and was an instant success.
_____c. play that Anna Cora believed had little value.
_____d. magazine that featured Anna Cora's articles.

3. First, Anna Cora gave dramatic readings. Then, she wrote a play. Next,
_____a. she married James Mowatt.
_____b. she began her acting career.
_____c. she joined a big city newspaper.
_____d. she went to Europe for her health.

4. The great female American writer
_____a. helped her husband avoid financial collapse.
_____b. relied upon her husband to support her.
_____c. lived a sheltered life, removed from reality.
_____d. was unaware of her capabilities and talent.

5. The American public of the 19th century
_____a. was interested in strictly American talent.
_____b. loved the theater and enjoyed famous actors.
_____c. rarely read plays; only novels from Europe.
_____d. was narrow-minded and extremely critical.

6. The name of Anna Cora Mowatt was associated with
_____a. strange happenings.
_____b. respectability.
_____c. scientific events.
_____d. European fashion.

7. When Anna Cora was a little girl, she
_____a. and her brothers and sisters would perform plays.
_____b. dreamed of becoming a famous actress in Europe.
_____c. worked hard and studied to be a lawyer.
_____d. wanted to please her parents more than anything else.

8. Anna Cora Mowatt thought that the manager of the Park Theater wanted her to become an actress because she
_____a. was very talented.
_____b. had a famous name.
_____c. was a curiosity.
_____d. was very popular.

9. Another name for this selection could be
_____a. "Changing Times."
_____b. "A Day to Remember."
_____c. "A New Fashion."
_____d. "Love and Marriage."

10. This selection is mainly about
_____a. a talented woman who was ahead of her time.
_____b. an actress who becomes rich and famous.
_____c. a marriage that withstands a great deal of pressure.
_____d. a family that encouraged their children to act.

11.   *Develop your own sentences using any four key words found in the box on the following page.*

1. _____
2. _____
3. _____
4. _____

Check your answers with the key on page 53.

FIRST AND FOREMOST

VOCABULARY CHECK

audition	champagne	diction	disapprove	encore	undertone

I.   Fill in the blank in each sentence with the correct key word from the box above.

1. Jean wanted to _____ for the part of Juliet in the school play.
2. We toasted Dad's new promotion with _____.
3. Because of her perfect _____, we loved to hear her recite poetry.
4. The audience shouted so loudly, that the actor had to return for an _____.
5. During the church service, Paul spoke to his wife in an _____.
6. Frank did not _____ of the idea, so they all voted for it.

II.   Fill in the blanks in the puzzle with the key words from the box.

Across

1. manner of speaking
2. a bubbly wine
3. an extra performance

Down

1. show dislike
4. to try out for a part in a play
5. something spoken in a quiet manner

Check your answers with the key on page 58.

There's No Place Like Dome

Learn the Key Words

arbitrary	(är′ bə trer ē)	not going by rule or law; determined by chance *His decision to sentence the boy to prison was not an <u>arbitrary</u> one.*
comparable	(kom′ pər ə bəl)	able to be compared; similar *This course is <u>comparable</u> to one I took last semester.*
contemporary	(kən tem′ pə rer ē)	having to do with the present; modern *Their furniture is a <u>contemporary</u> style.*
contour	(kon′ tu̇r)	the outline or shape of a figure *The <u>contour</u> of the island is very irregular.*
ingenious	(in jē′ nyəs)	good at inventing; cleverly planned or made *That architect has come up with some <u>ingenious</u> plans.*
tangible	(tan′ jə bəl)	real; something that can be touched *The improvements for their home are definitely <u>tangible</u>.*

Preview:

1. Read the title.
2. Look at the picture.
3. Read the first two paragraphs of the selection.
4. Then answer the following question.

You learned from your preview that

____a. Fuller's idea would be expensive and impractical.
____b. domes require unusual materials which are hard to find.
____c. the dome is basically a triangular shape.
____d. Fuller's hardest task was to prove the dome was tangible.

Turn to the Comprehension Check on page 39 for the right answer.

Now read the selection.

Read to find out about a practical alternative to modern buildings.

There's No Place Like Dome

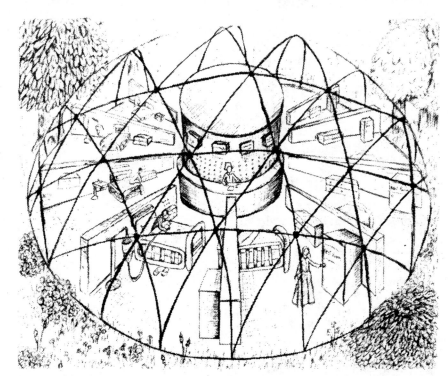

Unique, functional, convenient and economical—a perfect description of the latest trend in building. The dome is here to stay!

The world of the dome is a contemporary and unique one. Created by Buckminster Fuller, the dome is an unusual type of bubble building that defies almost all conventional building methods. Fuller's intent was to offer the most space by using the least amount of materials and labor. The ingenious inventor succeeded at this, but his most difficult task was convincing others that his idea was, indeed, tangible.

Fuller realized that there was nothing new about the dome. Nature displayed the dome shape in caves, bubbles, and even in certain insect's eyes. Fuller's domes would be comparable to these as well as to igloos, which are domes made from chunks of packed snow. There just had to be a practical way of designing, building and selling the dome. In order to sustain his vision, Fuller knew that he had to devise his own type of geometry, but it could not be an arbitrary shape and it had to deal with the spherical shape in a realistic way. Fuller divided the surface of a half sphere into triangles since the triangle is the strongest geometric shape. The sides of these triangles were to be as equal as possible. In this way, the structure would have even more strength.

Through his experiments, Fuller saw that within the arrangement of the triangles there existed a certain pulling force or tension, and this tension would be able to support the framework of the entire dome-shaped building. The amazing thing about this structure was that Fuller would not support his building with boards that were placed next to each other. The frame of his dome would be made up of many triangles that would curve back into each other. Each triangle was attached to the next and would help to support the other. They depended upon each other to sustain any load, such as wind, rain or snow. The construction was not arbitrary and would enable the load to be spread out evenly over the entire surface of the dome. The material out of which the dome was built seemed almost unimportant. As long as it was designed correctly, a dome could be made out of paper!

In the beginning, all of Fuller's theories fell on deaf ears. No specialist or scientist would believe that such a light, smoothly contoured, mobile structure could be tangible. But no one could subdue Fuller's desire to see his dream come true. Finally, after many trips to various college campuses and after many experiments, his new invention began to receive the attention that it deserved. It was a new awakening. Within the realm of the dome, Buckminster Fuller had become king. It was a new way to live in wide open space. It was for this method of enclosing space that Fuller applied for a patent from the United States government in 1951, and when he finally received it in 1954, his big break had already occurred.

The first big dome was constructed in 1953 for the Ford Motor Company at Henry Ford II's request. Fuller was called upon to devise a lightweight dome structure to be placed atop the Ford Rotunda building. His creation was an aluminum dome weighing twenty times less than a comparable conventional steel structure weighed. In addition to its light weight, the dome took only a record-breaking four months to construct and people came from all over the country to look up through the marvelous cobweb-type pattern. It was really quite an attraction.

Since that time many different variations of domes have been built for almost every kind of use. In dome talk, the supports that make up the frame of triangles are called *struts,* and the pieces that hold the struts together at cross points are called *hubs.* The struts, hubs, coverings and liners for domes are made of so many different materials and combinations that it would be impossible to explore them all. Yet although it sounds complicated, the dome is a masterpiece of simplicity. Perhaps a look at some of the most commonly used and contemporary types will inspire new creators.

The wood dome is comparable to the conventional house. The frame of the dome is made of wood and only the hubs are metal. The dome can easily be covered with boards or shingles. The heat and electricity might be any of the kinds found in usual homes, but solar energy might be a good alternative since it is both convenient and efficient. The wood dome is sometimes built on a platform or deck. This raises the dome and gives it a beautiful and different look, in addition to protecting it from decaying.

The wood dome is not always used as a home, however. A good example of another use for this dome is the Information Center at the Boston Children's Zoo.

The metal shell and plastic tension liner domes seem to have the most uses. The metal shell shines like a knight's armor and a plastic liner is attached to the frame at various hub points. The liner stays in place because it is pulled tightly. The plastic liner dome is very lightweight and can be put up on any hard surface. It can even be built on top of a roof.

There are no definite walls inside the dome so the rooms can be arranged wherever they are wanted. Heating units can even be hung from the ceiling to provide additional floor space. Sometimes this particular dome behaves in a peculiar manner. As night falls,

one might hear the metal shell make a crackling noise. This is because changes in temperature cause the shell to either expand or contract. You will experience another odd happening if you stand in the center of this dome and speak. Much to your surprise your voice will sound hollow to you. This is surely a funny feeling, but dome owners don't seem to mind. As a matter of fact, you become accustomed to it very quickly. Some examples of the most common uses for metal shell and plastic liner domes are gyms, classrooms, greenhouses and recreation centers. This type of dome can even be expanded to enclose rectangular objects such as built-in pools, tennis courts or shopping centers.

One of the most contemporary uses for the dome is as a medical center. This is a specially made dome that is noted for its mobility and simplicity of construction. The outside comes in durable plastic, triangular pieces and even the inside walls, equipment and furniture are part of some packages. Because the dome's contour is curved, people do not seem to feel they are in the usual kind of hospital or medical center. This seems to make them feel more relaxed. There is less wasted space and since the rooms are arranged in a circle, doctors and nurses can observe their patients more closely from the center.

Some of the most famous and unique domes are scattered around the world. Their contours are beautiful and most are simple and fast to construct. Some are even less than the cost of the usual building. The dome is not only an ingenious breakthrough in architecture, but also an unusual alternative to the ordinary outlook on life. It may take a while to adapt to this style of living, yet dome owners who have tried it refuse to stray from the realm of dome living. They seem to have found that there's just no place like dome.

There's No Place Like Dome

COMPREHENSION CHECK

Choose the best answer.

1. The individual responsible for originating the dome is
___a. Henry Ford II.
___b. Bernard Fuller.
___c. Benjamin Miller.
___d. Buckminster Fuller.

2. At first, specialists and scientists
___a. were thrilled at his idea.
___b. were skeptical about his idea.
___c. wanted to follow his practices.
___d. copied his outlines with care.

3. This selection leads us to believe that
___a. the dome is a practical concept.
___b. the dome is quite impractical.
___c. the dome was a complete failure.
___d. only one type of dome is practical.

4. The first major dome was constructed in
___a. 1853.
___b. 1935.
___c. 1953.
___d. 1963.

5. When you stand in the center of a dome,
___a. your voice can't be heard by others.
___b. you will have difficulty in seeing others.
___c. your ears will hurt from what you hear.
___d. your words will sound hollow to you.

6. The author's purpose for writing this story was to
___a. list the steps for building a dome.
___b. explain interesting facts about a dome.
___c. describe the problems of Fuller.
___d. prove domes are ridiculously inexpensive.

7. A contemporary use of the dome is as a
___a. mobile army base.
___b. center for research.
___c. medical center.
___d. home for the aged.

8. According to the selection,
___a. the uses for the dome are increasing.
___b. the uses for the dome are decreasing.
___c. scientists are still unwilling to use domes.
___d. the dome is not suitable for recreational purposes.

9. Another name for this selection could be
___a. "The Life of Buckminster Fuller."
___b. "Domes—A New Concept in Building."
___c. "Architecture in the 1950's."
___d. "New Homes for Eskimos."

10. This selection is mainly about
___a. problems in constructing domes.
___b. a unique type of building.
___c. places where domes are used.
___d. the materials in a dome.

11. *Develop your own sentences using any four key words found in the box on the following page.*

1 _____
2 _____
3 _____
4 _____

Check your answers with the key on page 53.

There's No Place Like Dome

VOCABULARY CHECK

| arbitrary | comparable | contemporary | contour | ingenious | tangible |

1. Fill in the blank in each sentence with the correct key word from the box above.

1. The sun is _____ to the moon because they both illuminate the earth.
2. From the plane, we could see the irregular _____ of the North American coast.
3. Whenever he played chess, his moves were _____.
4. Benjamin Franklin was an _____ inventor, as well as a printer, scholar and statesman.
5. _____ clothing is quite different from styles 70 years ago.
6. Inventors are always trying to prove that their ideas are _____

II. The key words are hidden in the group of letters below. They may be written across or up and down. Circle the key words. One word, that is not a key word, has been done for you.

```
S U A C I L H E A R T Y
B L U O N A V M N J L D
D U M N G A D N O T A R
C O N T E M P O R A R Y
Q R T O N D A D V N B L
A V L U I R L M O G I P
D F L R O P S D E I T T
B N O R U T H M L B R M
D A E I S O U B C L A S
C O M P A R A B L E R R
L J C E F L G Q T P Y A
```

Check your answers with the key on page 58.

The Fat Eaters

Learn the Key Words

capitalize	(kap′ ə tə līz)	to use to one's advantage or profit; to benefit from *In school, Mike learned to capitalize on his mistakes.*
coincide	(kō in sīd′)	correspond exactly; happen at the same time *Did your getting poor grades at school coincide with your illness?*
counteract	(koun′ tər akt)	act against; neutralize the effects of *There is no drug to counteract the effects of the poison.*
crave	(krāv)	desire strongly; want very much *I cannot lose weight because I crave sweets constantly.*
disfigure	(dis fig′ yər)	spoil the appearance of *The chemicals in the laboratory can disfigure you if they are not handled properly.*
tolerate	(tol′ ə rāt)	allow or permit; endure *The old man could not tolerate loud music.*

Preview:
1. Read the title.
2. Look at the picture.
3. Read the first eight paragraphs of the selection.
4. Then answer the following question.

You learned from your preview that
____a. people in Santa Margarita developed a new bacteria to "eat" fat.
____b. people in Santa Margarita became thin due to an accident.
____c. only thin people could live in Santa Margarita.
____d. Linda lost her excess weight only a few days ago.

Turn to the Comprehension Check on page 44 for the right answer.

Now read the selection.

Read to find out about a "battle" between science and nature.

The Fat Eaters

When the cargo of an oil tanker is accidentally spilled into the ocean, a drastic chain of events follow.

"I want the 'Banana Surprise' with five scoops of ice cream, whipped cream, chocolate syrup and sprinkles," said the chubby little girl, her voice dancing with excitement.

"Oh Annie dear, that's too much for you, and besides, you'll get very fat," her double-chinned mother answered.

"Oh come on, Betty," her husband interrupted, "let her enjoy herself. Remember we're in Santa Margarita, the place where people become slender no matter how much they eat. Isn't that correct, Miss?" The middle-aged man patted his potbelly and smiled at Linda, who was patiently waiting for their order.

"That's right," she responded, pivoting around quickly to show off her beautifully proportioned figure.

The woman sighed, saying, "When I was a teenager, I too, was almost as thin as you."

"But I was plump until the fat eaters came," Linda replied.

"Fat eaters?" the couple asked.

"Yes," Linda continued. "A couple of years ago oil tankers accidentally spilled some of their cargo in the ocean and countless sea animals and birds died. Scientists then created bacteria to eat the oil and released it into the sea. The oil disappeared in a short time. My weight loss happened to coincide with that event. Now I can eat anything without gaining weight. Everyone who stays here for a little while loses weight without trying."

Enthused by this suggestion, the man ordered the fanciest desserts on the menu for his family, and before leaving, tipped Linda generously, adding, "You have the world's best ice cream, which we'll crave forever."

Linda's parents owned the ice cream parlor and purchased products which were sold elsewhere in the United States, but they tasted more delicious in Santa Margarita because people did not fear gaining weight. Linda's parents had recently decided to capitalize on their town's fame by enlarging and redecorating the parlor which had been a modest gathering spot for local teenagers. Now it was a prosperous and elegant tourist attraction where Linda earned

enough to buy the car she wanted by working after school and on weekends.

After lunch, Linda prepared to leave and she got out of her uniform and into her jeans and t-shirt. With her long blond hair and slender figure, she was frequently mistaken for a Hollywood actress. Flattered, she tried to dress like one.

"I need another pair of jeans, Mom. I simply can't tolerate these baggy ones anymore," she told her mother.

"You're getting too thin. Eat before you go," her mother said.

"I have to hurry, Mom. Jim is waiting for me," Linda replied and drove off to the beach, where Jim worked as a lifeguard.

When she arrived, Jim was gazing intently toward the ocean through his field glasses, ignoring the girls who clustered around his chair. Linda knew that these girls were eager to show off their recently slimmed figures. The newcomers with pale, chubby bodies stared at the slender people and tried to guess which ones were natives.

"Hi, what are you looking at?"

Linda called out to Jim.

"Something strange is happening on Seal Rock," he answered, handing her the field glasses.

On the small rock island where seals sunned themselves on their southward migration from Alaska, there were numerous seals, as usual, but none moved. It was impossible that every animal's nap time should coincide with his neighbor's.

"Let's go out to the rock when you get off duty," Linda suggested.

They were on their way in about an hour. As they approached Seal Rock, Jim turned off the motor of the boat and started rowing in order to avoid disturbing the animals.

"The seals are dead!" Linda suddenly exclaimed. "And look how skinny they are!"

Hundreds of seals lay dead on the island, reduced almost to skeletons, and many other carcasses of both seals and fish in a similar condition floated on the surface of the water. She and Jim signaled to the Coast Guard cutter which they spotted nearby to report their findings.

"We know," the captain said, "but we cannot understand why they died, since there is definitely enough food for them in the ocean."

"Do you suppose that the fat eaters are responsible?" Linda questioned quietly, as she tightened the belt around her jeans that had become several sizes too big for her during the last few weeks. She added, "Maybe we'll end up like those seals."

Jim looked up, startled.

"Nonsense," he said forcing a smile. "You are beautiful. But eat more or you'll disappear."

"You should take your own advice," Linda retorted.

Without answering, Jim started the motor. Linda realized that she hit a raw nerve. Jim's once developed muscles were wasting away.

"I'm sorry," she said softly.

A week later, when the plump family returned to the ice cream parlor, looking radiant with greatly slimmed bodies, they mistook Linda for her mother. Tearfully, Linda ran to the mirror

and admitted to herself for the first time that her skin hung loose and wrinkled all over her face and body. What could disfigure her so?

"You are exhausted dear, and losing too much weight. Take a day off," her mother suggested consolingly.

Linda stayed away from school and her job for a whole week, hiding from her friends and trying desperately to regain her energy. She ate whatever she craved and her jaws ached from eating constantly. She took medication to gain weight, but nothing seemed to counteract the reducing process. She avoided the mirror, for she could not tolerate her reflection. She was increasingly convinced that the seals' unhappy fate awaited her, too. In fact, the horrible doom hung over the whole town. Then, she wondered why her parents and the mayor never lost weight. As tourists fled the town, scientists arrived to study the problem.

One afternoon when Linda was sitting in the garden, a skinny old man greeted her.

"Don't you recognize me anymore?" he pleaded.

"Jim!" she cried. "I thought you were ignoring me because you couldn't tolerate the sight of me."

"I was embarrassed to show myself," Jim admitted.

"Vanity," they said giggling, and entered the kitchen to share the mountain of food that Linda's mother had left.

Scientists soon discovered that the oil-eating bacteria invaded the bodies of sea animals and devoured their fat after they finished off the oil spilled in the sea. People who swam in the sea or ate fish naturally absorbed the bacteria, which disfigured them. Scientists also feared that the fat eaters would attack the oil reserves under the ground, too.

"So my parents and the mayor escaped because they hate fish and never swim," Linda concluded, "and soon they will be the only ones left in the town."

To change the subject, Jim turned on the television.

"We interrupt this program to bring you an important

announcement," the announcer said. "Another bacteria that destroys the fat eaters has been discovered," he continued, "and it is being released into the sea at this moment. Everyone exposed to the original bacteria is urged to report immediately to the Public Health office for an injection of the counteracting bacteria."

"Thank God for brilliant scientists," Jim sighed.

"Don't be so sure," said Linda, quietly.

The remedy worked wonders—everyone gained weight, felt stronger and looked younger. The town capitalized on the latest discovery by setting up a clinic where people would get an injection of the fat eaters to lose weight and its antidote to gain back weight whenever necessary. Tourists from all over the world flocked to Santa Margarita again to keep in shape without really trying and Linda made enough money to pay for her entire college education. One day as she drove to the beach and tiptoed over the hot sand to the lifeguard's chair, Jim greeted her with a scream. Linda's hair had blown away with the wind and she was completely bald! Jim's transistor radio, which fell into the sand, kept repeating the announcement, "Important! Scientists have just discovered that the new bacteria created to destroy the fat eaters, has a side effect..."

The Fat Eaters

COMPREHENSION CHECK

Choose the best answer.

1. The fat eaters were created to help
   _____a. clean sewage from the sea.
   _____b. people lose weight.
   _____c. clear up an oil spill.
   _____d. help cure a terrible disease.

2. People went to Santa Margarita because
   _____a. the seafood was delicious.
   _____b. they could eat as much as they wanted and still lose weight.
   _____c. the ice cream parlor made fantastic sundaes.
   _____d. Linda was a famous movie star.

[3.] Bacteria is a
   _____a. dangerous substance with which to experiment.
   _____b. helpful substance that never has negative results.
   _____c. cure for all types of dangerous diseases.
   _____d. safe solution to a pollution problem.

4. The people in this selection
   _____a. preferred artificial methods to regulate their eating habits.
   _____b. enjoyed dieting and keeping in good physical health.
   _____c. moderated their eating habits through a disciplined program.
   _____d. benefited greatly from their visit to the town of Santa Margarita.

5. The residents of Santa Margarita were
   _____a. undernourished, but happy.
   _____b. fond of easy solutions.
   _____c. concerned about the future.
   _____d. uneducated, but attractive.

Preview Answer:
b. people in Santa Margarita became thin due to an accident.

---

6. First, the scientists released the fat eaters into the ocean. Then, certain residents began to lose weight drastically. Next,
   _____a. people began to lose their hair.
   _____b. scientists created and released a new bacteria.
   _____c. residents returned to their original weights.
   _____d. visitors returned to their homes in despair.

7. Scientists created a new bacteria to
   _____a. replenish the fish.
   _____b. clean up Seal Rock.
   _____c. become famous.
   _____d. devour the fat eaters.

8. Linda was
   _____a. compassionate and sensitive.
   _____b. self-absorbed and insensitive.
   _____c. always delighted with her appearance.
   _____d. able to accept her fate calmly.

9. Another name for this selection could be
   _____a. "Advanced Technology."
   _____b. "Easy Remedies May Backfire."
   _____c. "A Resort Town."
   _____d. "Pollution Control."

10. This selection is mainly about
   _____a. the life of an active young girl.
   _____b. a place where people stay thin.
   _____c. a cycle in which problems are created by a solution.
   _____d. science, its progress and achievements in the last century.

11. *Develop your own sentences using any four key words found in the box on the following page.*

1 _____
2 _____
3 _____
4 _____

Check your answers with the key on page 53.

The Fat Eaters

VOCABULARY CHECK

capitalize	coincide	counteract	crave	disfigure	tolerate

I. Choose the correct key word from the box above to complete the following sentences.

1. John's outgoing personality helped to _____ the tense atmosphere at the party.

2. One must learn to _____ on the opportunities that are offered.

3. Susan's arrival will _____ with our plans to see the afternoon show.

4. Sometimes I _____ rich, chewy chocolate bars.

5. The teacher would no longer _____ Paul's rude behavior in class.

6. Be careful while working with acid, since it could _____ your features.

II. Choose the six key words to complete the following paragraph. When you are finished, you will have a brief account of the story.

Many of the residents of Santa Margarita could eat anything they wanted and not gain weight. This incredible event happened to _____ with an oil spill. Scientists remedied the problem by releasing an oil-eating bacteria into the ocean. The residents decided to _____ on this event. They directed their attention to those people who would _____ thin bodies more than anything else. Soon there was no controlling the weight loss and people were frantic. They could _____ the problem no more. No one ever realized that the bacteria could _____ them so, and soon scientists developed a new bacteria to _____ the ill effects of the first one. The results of this creation were even more dramatic than the original.

Check your answers with the key on page 59.

Evidence of the Impossible

Learn the Key Words

audible (ô′ də bəl) loud enough to be heard
The distant sound of a motor was clearly audible.

foreboding (for bō′ ding) a feeling that something bad is going to happen
He had a strong foreboding that all was not well.

illusion (i lü′ zhən) a false impression
Although surrounded by danger, he had created the illusion of safety.

perceive (per sēv′) to know or understand through the senses
I could perceive that she was angry, in spite of her denials.

spouse (spous) a husband or wife
She and her spouse had been married thirty years.

supernatural (sü pər nach′ ər əl) that which cannot be explained by natural laws; frequently involving ghosts or spirits
Supernatural events are often difficult to believe.

Preview:
1. Read the title.
2. Look at the picture.
3. Read the first three paragraphs of the selection.
4. Then answer the following question.

You learned from your preview that
_____a. Jody lived with her grandparents.
_____b. the story is an autobiography.
_____c. the author believes that Jody had a supernatural experience.
_____d. the story takes place on the last day of Christmas.

Turn to the Comprehension Check on page 49 for the right answer.

Now read the selection.

Read to find out about the possibility of another world.

Evidence of the Impossible

We live in a physical world where things can either be explained or proven. Yet, beyond this reality, there may be a spiritual world which defies all natural laws.

Jody is a sensible person as well as a trusted friend who insists her story is true, and I have no reason to doubt her. Can you accept her account of the supernatural, with its unusual sequence of events and the meager evidence that it did, indeed, happen? You may conclude that it was simply illusion, since, after all, you don't know Jody. I met her when we were both young children, at about the time, in fact, of her supernatural experience. Now, I will offer you her story, exactly as she related it to me, and you may judge for yourself.

Outside, an icy wind whipped powdery snow into crazy patterns. It rattled the windows and whistled down the chimney, fanning the flames higher and scattering a few embers out over the hearth, where they glowed briefly, then died.

Jody snuggled deeper into the big chair where she sat beside her grandmother. The house was cozy and Jody was contented as they talked quietly, drowsy before the fire, sipping hot cocoa. Jody was seven, spending part of her Christmas vacation with her grandparents, and she talked of toys and candy and Christmas morning. Her grandmother's talk was much of the same. Neither had the slightest foreboding about the night to come. The events they would remember the rest of their lives would take them completely by surprise.

The hall clock began to chime and Jody silently counted along, raising a finger for each chime. She used up all ten fingers and two of her bare toes.

"Twelve o'clock, so Grandpa won't be coming for two more hours," she announced in a sleepy mumble.

"Suppose we can make it, Boots?" her grandmother whispered. It was easy to perceive that she was sleepy, too.

Jody delayed answering the question as she fidgeted, gazing at her bare feet stretched toward the comforting warmth of the fire. Even as a baby she had preferred bare feet and had stubbornly kicked off any booties that dared cover them. That was how she got the nickname "Boots." She wiggled her toes and answered her grandmother's question with a question of her own.

"Can you stay awake, Grandma?"

"I'm afraid not," was the weary reply.

Jody thought a moment, fighting disappointment. She knew sleep was overtaking her, but she hated to admit it.

"Well," the little girl sighed, "we sure tried." Her grandmother chuckled and offered some comfort, saying, "Don't feel bad, Boots. In all the years your grandpa has worked the night shift, I don't believe I've managed to wait up for him more than a half dozen times. He'll understand."

"Maybe tomorrow night?" Jody suggested.

"Sure, we can try again tomorrow night," her grandmother agreed, giving Jody a small hug.

The fire was dying and the prospect of a warm bed was inviting to both sleepy people. They wandered into the kitchen to deposit their empty cups in the sink. Her grandmother got out a blue china cup and a little pan and placed them on the counter, next to the cocoa. On such a chilly night, her husband often made himself a cup of cocoa so he could warm up and relax before going to bed. Jody and her grandmother determined that both doors were securely locked and, leaving the usual light glowing in the living room, the two slowly ascended the stairs. Grandma tucked Jody into bed and the little girl fell instantly asleep. Then the woman went to her own room, slid gratefully beneath the covers, and drifted off to sleep.

During the next several hours all was silent, except for the audible ticking of the clock in the downstairs hallway and the occasional rattle of the windows. One o'clock arrived and departed with a solitary chime.

Jody awoke as the clock chimed two. She knew her grandfather could easily walk home from work in fifteen minutes, but in this weather, it would take about twenty. She drifted off almost immediately after the chime, waking again when she heard the key in the lock. The front door squeaked open, then squeaked shut. She anticipated the familiar sound of stamping feet knocking snow from boots, but it didn't come before Jody went back to sleep. She awoke one more time to familiar sounds that came from the kitchen. She smiled, knowing Grandpa was making his cocoa. Again, she slept, not waking until later, when the doorbell rang.

Jody's grandmother didn't hear the key in the lock nor the squeaking of the door because she was sleeping quite heavily. For some unknown reason, she did awaken to the noises in the kitchen. She could perceive the audible click of a spoon against china and the dull scraping of a pan being placed in the sink. She decided to go downstairs and sit with her spouse while he finished his cocoa, but sleep reclaimed her before she could move. Her sleep was not deep and she awoke when the light above the stairs snapped on. Her back was to the door, but the light shone on the wall she was facing. The stairs creaked audibly from the weight of the climber, then the light

snapped off and all was dark as he came into the room. She drifted off again until the bed was jiggled by the familiar weight settling beside her. She turned to say a few words to her husband and kiss him good night. His side of the bed was empty.

Surprised and confused, she had limited time to wonder because someone was ringing the front doorbell. As she scrambled into her robe and slippers, she decided she had been dreaming, that the sights and sounds had obviously been illusions. This would be her husband, now; apparently, he'd forgotten his key. She smiled at the thought, since Jack prided himself on his reliable memory.

She had nearly reached the stairs before she was aware of a curious situation. The house was completely dark. What had happened to the living room light? She switched on the light over the stairs and hurried down to the living room. When she reached the lamp and tried the switch, the light came on, as always. It had simply been turned off. When? By whom? The incident made her uneasy and she would have to find a good explanation but, for the moment, the bell was still ringing and Jack must be getting cold and impatient, she thought. Quickly, she unlocked the door and opened it to find, not her spouse, but a police officer. The sight filled her with foreboding, but she invited him in.

The story the policeman told was a simple one. Jack had been walking home, just after two o'clock, and was crossing a street. Because of the blinding snow, the driver of a truck hadn't seen him until too late. He hit the brakes, but the truck slid into the icy intersection and struck Jack. An ambulance was called, but it was useless; Jack had died instantly. Information in Jack's wallet had identified him, but an official identification would have to be made, and the officer explained to Jody's grandmother that she or another relative would have to do it as soon as possible. He quietly suggested that she contact friends or relatives to help her through the coming few days, offered awkward but sincere sympathy, and asked if he could

do anything for her.

In disbelief and confusion, the woman slowly turned away from the policeman. Jody stood at the bottom of the staircase, having been awakened by the commotion and having heard the tragic report, but she was not looking at her grandmother. Instead, her gaze was fixed on an object on the coffee table before the fireplace. The woman's gaze followed her granddaughter's.

As the wind rattled the windows and the clock ticked away those first moments of grief, the two remaining members of the household stared at a blue china cup, half filled with cocoa.

The following day, the dead man was officially identified as Jody's grandfather. He had never reached his destination. Or had he?

Evidence of the Impossible

COMPREHENSION CHECK

Choose the best answer.

1. Jody
   ____a. went to get the police on the night of her grandfather's death.
   ____b. waited up all night for her grandfather to come home.
   ____c. told her story to the author when they were both young children.
   ____d. wrote about the story just as it happened to her.

2. Before the policeman arrived, Jody and her grandmother
   ____a. were sure that Jack was home.
   ____b. had a strange foreboding about Jack.
   ____c. had an anxious sleep and bad dreams.
   ____d. were feeling depressed and lonely.

3. Jody's grandmother
   ____a. enjoyed making up stories.
   ____b. was a loving, sensible woman.
   ____c. was known for imagining things.
   ____d. was always afraid without her husband around.

4. According to the selection, which of the following statements does *not* support the idea of Jody's grandfather's return home?
   ____a. A dark living room.
   ____b. A half-empty cup of cocoa.
   ____c. A policeman at the door.
   ____d. A sound from the kitchen.

5. The author
   ____a. knows that other people have had similar experiences.
   ____b. feels that some people will not believe the story.
   ____c. does not trust such a young girl as a source.
   ____d. will never believe in supernatural experiences.

6. First, Jody's grandmother was aware of a light being turned on and then off. Then, she felt the bed sink down next to her. Next,
   ____a. she turned to find no one there.
   ____b. she went downstairs to find her husband in the kitchen.
   ____c. she ran in to check on Jody.
   ____d. she turned off the light in the living room.

7. The policeman came to the house because
   ____a. he wanted to warn Jody and her grandmother of a storm.
   ____b. there had been a burglar in the house.
   ____c. he wanted shelter from the storm.
   ____d. Jody's grandfather was killed by a truck.

8. From the evidence in the story,
   ____a. one is able to justify the entire incident, simply.
   ____b. it seemed that Jody's grandfather had returned home.
   ____c. one can deduce that it was only their imaginations.
   ____d. it was obvious that the man never came home.

9. Another name for this selection might be
   ____a. "Wishing and Hoping."
   ____b. "Only a Dream."
   ____c. "A Deep Sleep."
   ____d. "A Strange Winter's Night."

10. This selection is mainly about
   ____a. a terrible accident on a stormy night.
   ____b. a Christmas vacation at Jody's grandparents' house.
   ____c. an event that is unexplainable and mysterious.
   ____d. a girl named Boots and her young friend.

11. *Develop your own sentences using any four key words found in the box on the following page.*
   1 _____
   2 _____
   3 _____
   4 _____

Check your answers with the key on page 53.

Evidence of the Impossible

VOCABULARY CHECK

audible	foreboding	illusion	perceive	spouse	supernatural

I. Fill in the blank in each sentence with the correct key word from the box above.

1. The volume of the radio was so low, it was barely _____.

2. Her _____ entered the living room, carrying the morning paper.

3. _____ events are almost impossible to explain.

4. The heat rising from the pavement gave the _____ of a wet surface.

5. We could _____ that her mood was one of depression.

6. Christopher spoke in horror of his _____ as he approached the deserted house.

II. Your key words are listed in Column A. The definitions are in Column B. On each line in Column A write the letter of the correct definition.

Column A	Column B
____1. foreboding	a. something that can be heard
____2. supernatural	b. to know or understand through the senses
____3. spouse	c. a false impression
____4. perceive	d. a husband or a wife
____5. illusion	e. that which cannot be explained by natural laws
____6. audible	f. a strong sense of coming misfortune

Check your answers with the key on page 59.

KEY WORDS
Lessons I-21 — I-30

I-21

amputate
belligerent
concede
converge
decisive
ravage

I-22

antagonize
arrogant
comply
deliberate
fatality
suppress

I-23

bewitch
famished
hoodwink
lust
secrete
siesta

I-24

aroma
captivate
contemplate
denounce
disciple
regime

I-25

compress
consecutive
disrupt
prism
propel
serene

I-26

coordination
dejected
disqualify
lament
stress
wistful

KEY WORDS
Lessons I-21 — I-30

I-27

audition
champagne
diction
disapprove
encore
undertone

I-28

arbitrary
comparable
contemporary
contour
ingenious
tangible

I-29

capitalize
coincide
counteract
crave
disfigure
tolerate

I-30

audible
foreboding
illusion
perceive
spouse
supernatural

COMPREHENSION CHECK ANSWER KEY
Lessons I-21 — I-30

LESSON NUMBER	QUESTION NUMBER										PAGE NUMBER
	1	2	3	4	5	6	7	8	9	10	
I-21	c	b	◇c	c	a	○c	[a]	b	△a	□a	4
I-22	a	○a	b	[c]	◇a	d	b	a	△c	□a	9
I-23	b	d	b	○b	○d	[b]	◇a	d	△d	□c	14
I-24	c	a	○d	b	○a	[c]	◇b	b	△a	□b	19
I-25	a	○b	a	○b	[a]	[d]	○c	○b	△a	□b	24
I-26	a	○d	[b]	a	◇c	b	c	○b	△d	□b	29
I-27	○c	a	◇b	○a	[d]	b	a	c	△c	□a	34
I-28	d	b	○a	◇c	d	[b]	c	○a	△b	□b	39
I-29	c	b	[a]	a	○b	◇b	d	○b	△b	□c	44
I-30	c	a	○b	c	○b	◇a	d	[b]	△d	□c	49

Code: ○ = Inference

◇ = Sequence

[ ] = Critical Judgement

△ = Another Name for the Selection

□ = Main Idea

NOTES

VOCABULARY CHECK ANSWER KEY
Lessons I-21—I-30

I-21   **FULL STEAM AHEAD!**   5

I.
1. amputate
2. ravage
3. belligerent
4. concede
5. converge
6. decisive

II.
1. Yes
2. Yes
3. No
4. No
5. Yes
6. Yes

I-22   **THE MARKET STREET MASSACRE**   *II.*   10

I.
1. antagonize
2. arrogant
3. suppress
4. fatality
5. comply
6. deliberate

```
                    ²S
         ¹C         U
         O          P
         M          P
         P          R
⁴D E L I B E R ³A T E
         Y    S    N
              S    T
                   A
        ⁵A R R O G A N T
                   O
                   N
        ⁶F A T A L I T Y
                   Z
                   E
```

VOCABULARY CHECK ANSWER KEY
Lessons I-21 — I-30

I-23 **THE YELLOW ROSE OF TEXAS**

I.
1. famished
2. entice
3. hoodwink
4. lust
5. secrete
6. siesta

II.
1. Yes
2. Yes
3. No
4. Yes
5. No
6. No

I-24 **THE LORD OF THE MOUNTAIN**

20

I.
1. captivate
2. regime
3. aroma
4. denounce
5. contemplate
6. disciple

II.

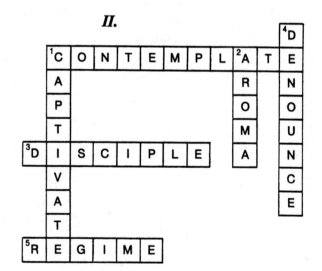

56

VOCABULARY CHECK ANSWER KEY
Lessons I-21 — I-30

I-25   THE END OF EDEN   25

I.		II.	
1.	serene	1.	c
2.	consecutive	2.	d
3.	disrupt	3.	e
4.	propel	4.	b
5.	compress	5.	f
6.	prism	6.	a

I-26   RACE THE CHUCKWAGONS   30

I.		II.	
1.	coordination	1.	d
2.	dejected	2.	c
3.	disqualify	3.	a
4.	stress	4.	b
5.	lament	5.	c
6.	wistful	6.	a

LESSON NUMBER

PAGE NUMBER

I-27 FIRST AND FOREMOST

35

I.
1. audition
2. champagne
3. diction
4. encore
5. undertone
6. disapprove

II.

	¹D	I	C	T	I	O	N	
	I							
	S					⁵U		
²C	H	A	M	P	⁴A	G	N	E
	P				U	D		
	P				D	E		
	R				I	R		
	O				T	T		
	V				I	O		
	E				O	N		
	N			³E	N	C	O	R	E

I-28 THERE'S NO PLACE LIKE DOME

II.

40

I.
1. comparable
2. contour
3. arbitrary
4. ingenious
5. Contemporary
6. tangible

```
S  U  A  C  I  L  H  E  A  R  T  Y
B  L  U  O  N  A  V  M  N  J  L  D
D  U  M  N  G  A  D  N  O  T  A  R
C  O  N  T  E  M  P  O  R  A  R  Y
Q  R  T  O  N  D  A  D  V  N  B  L
A  V  L  U  I  R  L  M  O  G  I  P
D  F  L  R  O  P  S  D  E  I  T  T
B  N  O  R  U  T  H  M  L  B  R  M
D  A  E  I  S  O  U  B  C  L  A  S
C  O  M  P  A  R  A  B  L  E  R  R
L  J  C  E  F  L  G  Q  T  P  Y  A
```

58

VOCABULARY CHECK ANSWER KEY
Lessons I-21 — I-30

I-29   **THE FAT EATERS**   45

I.   1. counteract
       2. capitalize
       3. coincide
       4. crave
       5. tolerate
       6. disfigure

II.   1. coincide
        2. capitalize
        3. crave
        4. tolerate
        5. disfigure
        6. counteract

I-30   **EVIDENCE OF THE IMPOSSIBLE**   50

I.   1. audible
       2. spouse
       3. Supernatural
       4. illusion
       5. perceive
       6. foreboding

II.   1. f
        2. e
        3. d
        4. b
        5. c
        6. a

NOTES